Selling Solutions

Selling Solutions

Over a Dozen Proven "Formulas" You Can Use to Focus Your Talents, Target Your Markets and Get Appointments with People Who Will Buy What You Offer

ROGER GERTZ, CLU

Selling Solutions
Over a Dozen Proven "Formulas" You Can Use to Focus Your Talents, Target Your Markets and Get Appointments with People Who Will Buy What You Offer

Printed in the United States of America.

Roger Gertz
VisCalc, LLC
roger@viscalc.com
770.422.3501
www.VisCalc.com

ISBN-13: 978-0692682982
ISBN-10: 0692682988

ENDORSEMENTS

"As President and CEO of Universal Guarantee Life Insurance Company, I was introduced to Roger Gertz by one of our leading agents. We wanted to develop a competitive edge by introducing unique market leader soft wear and distribute our products using a portable computer at point of sale. We were one of the first to do so. Roger provided us with both tools on a timely basis and at a price that was very competitive. We were able to triple the sales results in our company within a short period of time and Roger also became one of our leading producers in the process. He still holds the all-time record sale ... a $20Million face amount with a single premium of $6 million. *[Author's Note: Turn to chapter 13 to read this story.]*

"These results led to my promotion as Chief Marketing Officer of our parent company, Sun Life of America, working with Roger over many years at that company as well. He is exceptionally bright, understands the marketplace dynamics, honest and always delivered value added well beyond our expectations. His ability to provide sales oriented soft wear was enhanced because he understands how an agent thinks and can communicate his concepts in a manner that prospects understand as well.

"My forty-eight-year career in our great industry, and the success I was able to enjoy, would not have been possible without individuals like Roger."

KENNETH MLEKUSH, CLU
RETIRED PRESIDENT OF JEFFERSON PILOT LIFE

"My company was introduced to Roger Gertz three years ago from a business associate at another Fraternal Life Insurance Company. Words can't express the gratitude that I have for that introduction. The entire process of completely transforming our current illustration software to Roger's system was painless and very enlightening. Roger created not only a state of the art illustration system, but he also has a magnitude of insurance sales experience that he incorporated into the software as well.

"I find that Roger is always willing and eager to listen to new ideas and critiques to personalize this software for our organization's specific needs. I would be remiss if I didn't mention Roger's young genius, Josh DeBoer, who works in the background. He is an amazing programmer and his ability to understand the insurance industry from his side of the business at such a young age is truly a gift from God.

"In one statement: If you don't take a look at VisCalc for your illustration needs, you are truly holding back your organization!"

JOHN DENNING
SALES MANAGER, FRATERNAL LIFE COMPANY

"After my Army days, and different jobs I signed a contract with the Gleaner Life Insurance Society and started selling on part-time bases and after a year I became a full-time agent. A year later, the company moved me to Bowling Green, OH to become an agency manager. This was 1974 and 10 years later I found myself suffering in the insurance business with same old products and hardly enough income to live on.

"At this time with my low income, I qualified my children for the student lunch program from the government. We never used it but this told me I needed some help. That's when a good friend introduced me to Roger Gertz. Roger had a growing agency that was going crazy in the market. I found out that Gleaner Life was coming out with a Universal Life Product. He asked if I could introduce him to the president of the company. That was 1984 and with Roger's development of their illustration software and his sales guidance, they had at that time, their biggest year ever.

"1984 turned out to be the first year I ever made any real money and qualified with for a trip to London, England in 1985. I ended up bringing my whole family to England and stayed for three months. That year became my first 'six figure' income year.

"Roger became my manager. I think it was one of the best decisions I ever made. Thanks to him, all three of my children graduated from college. Thanks again."

GARY ANTHONY, RETIRED AGENT
GLEANER LIFE INSURANCE SOCIETY

TABLE OF CONTENTS

INTRODUCTION

I love this quote from the 18th century outlaw Jesse James. Supposedly a sheriff asked Jesse why he robbed banks, to which Jesse replied:

"Because that is where the money is!"

If you analyze what he said, it is actually profound. Now, being an 18th century outlaw, Jesse James probably said it to be a smart aleck. But as an insurance agent, know that *you must pursue people who have money to purchase your product*. Otherwise you are spinning your wheels. For instance, no one goes into the life insurance business and targets teenagers. They have about as much interest in life insurance as they do in a discussion about Social Security. That would be ridiculous.

In this book, my aim to is to help you discover and seize the markets where the money is. Over the years I have spoken with all sorts of people, from agents to company presidents. One question that inevitably reoccurs is, "Roger, you have always been a million-dollar producer. How did you reach that level?"

I always share the answer. And that is what this book is about.

At this point in my career, I feel obligated to give something back to our industry. And I am glad to do it. I want to pour into the industry that has been so good to me. Ignoring the financial aspect, I have gained many relationships with agents, managers, and company officers. These people are still my personal friends after many years.

Decades of my marketing and business experience are crammed into the pages of this book. You can digest a chapter at a time. In fact, I would even say this book is written in digestible bites. If you eat too much for dinner, you will feel stuffed and get a stomach ache. But if you take things in smaller bites—especially if you are eating a filet mignon—you can really savor the flavor. So this book is intentionally written in bite-sized chapters.

What sets me apart? Why should you heed my advice? Well, I have been a multimillion-dollar producer for years now. So you can rest assured that these tactics work.

And I have acquired somewhat of a reputation because of my involvement with computer-prepared illustrations. It is crazy how I got involved in the first place—if you had told me back then how much these illustrations would affect my career, I would have laughed at you.

In the old days at our little agency, there were four of us agents. We shared one secretary, a very fine gal. She was a wonderful typist, but to do an illustration on a typewriter could easily take her an hour or two. She had all the policy rates and values in "per thousand" numbers, so a $10,000 policy illustration was easy: move the decimal point one place. For a $100,000 policy, move the decimal point two places. But if it was a $25,000 policy, she had to multiply all the rates by 25! What a job!

Creating illustrations was hard, laborious work. She could be the fastest typist in the world, but she would be hard pressed to produce more than one illustration per day for each agent.

One day when I was riding with an associate, we stopped at a business in Pompano Beach where one of his friends worked. The business–Chris Craft Corporation–owned a big IBM 360 computer, which cost over $4 million. That is right, four million dollars! And this was years ago, when the dollar was worth a lot more. So it was an expensive machine. Sitting next to the huge air conditioning units (to remove the heat the computer generated), the IBM 360 was an impressive sight.

I was introduced to a fellow who did programming for the computer. When he demonstrated its capabilities, I could not believe what the computer was able to do. Never before had I seen anything like it. It could complete a calculation in a nanosecond. I paid the programmer to write a life insurance illustration program.

In those days, programs were entered into the computer using IBM cards. You are probably to young to have ever seen an IBM card. It was about six inches long and three inches wide. One of the corners is clipped off, and a bunch of rectangular holes are punched all over the card.

If you wanted the computer to create an illustration, you had to input the data through punched IBM cards. You would sit down at a desk holding a typewriter-like device. You would use the device to punch the IBM cards. If you made a mistake, you had to eject the card and redo that card.

When you finished creating your data, you had amassed a stack of IBM cards. The stack might be an inch thick, or it might be four inches thick. Whatever the size, you would take the stack of cards over to the processor person, who would load the cards into the computer. Usually, the computer was so fast and so underworked that the operation did not take more than a few seconds.

I ended up buying time on the computer. I paid a horrible price: $25 per hour for computer time. But the computer could execute my program in about five seconds. Since I was paying $25 each hour, each illustration cost me about 2¢ to produce. That was a steal.

The illustration printed out on what we called "pajama paper." It was big, wide paper with green and white stripes on it. The pajama paper changed my career, because it completely separated me from all the other agents. No one had ever made illustrations on IBM computer paper before, but Roger Gertz did. I just happened to stumble into that idea–no big brilliance on my part. I just wanted to see if my program would work. The operator said, "Well, we should try it out. Put a stack of that paper in the machine." Bingo! Out came the illustration. And it changed my life.

Gone were the days of our poor secretary typing for hours to produce an illustration. With computer technology having advanced to this point, we could produce an illustration in a few seconds. Before, I went into an appointment with one hopefully-saleable illustration. And I was not sure exactly what the prospect might be interested in. Now I could have four or even more illustrations! It would only take a few seconds to print each one.

Then lo and behold, in 1980, along came Steve Jobs with the Mac and Bill Gates with Microsoft to create programs for the IBM PC. Those innovations brought the computer down to the agent's level. Now a successful insurance agent could own a computer himself.

Considering those early days, I have to laugh. A computer and a printer easily cost $5,000. Today, you can get a computer that is 100 times faster and a high-tech laser printer, both for $500. The times, they are a-changin'.

That technology really moved the business. At my agency, we decided to "computerize" all our products. We took all the products the insurance companies offered and made them available in the software. We could select a product, type in the name and age, enter the dollar amount, press a button, and get the illustration.

When you have a solution that fast compared with typing, it frees up time to focus on selling solutions instead of pushing products. (We will explore this idea more in chapter two.)

I could spend my time concentrating on the most important question: "What is the proper solution for this prospect?" No longer was my time consumed by creating these sales illustrations. My emphasis shifted to the prospect: What solution fits them best?

Once I realized I had the technology to sell insurance, I had to figure out how to define my market. And that is what this book is mainly about.

As a result of the first illustration program I created for the IBM 360, over the years I have authored over 200 software programs. I have developed programs for many different insurance companies. Fortunately, I was one of the very early birds with the new technology. After a while, I became known for that ability in the business. I had companies contact me to help them with technology because they had heard about me. Or better yet, because a client of mine gave one of their agents an illustration I had created. The agent took the illustration to his company and said, "Look what these people have!" Then the company called me.

That continues to this day. Just two weeks ago, a company's vice president called me. He said, "An agent told us to call you, because you have the best software he has ever seen." I did not solicit that. The call came from 800 miles away! The vice president did not know me from Adam, but he called me right away when he saw what my software could do. I was in the right place at the right time with the right solution.

We will discuss software many times throughout this book. At the very end, I will share how you can get access to my many powerful software programs with a special offer. But first, we need to teach you how to sell solutions.

Roger Gertz
March 14, 2016

SECTION I.

PARADIGM SHIFT

WHAT DO YOU HAVE TO SELL?

As an overview, most agents have two basic products to sell: life insurance and annuities. These two products are quite different from each other, and it is worth looking at each product.

Life insurance is segregated into two forms of insurance. The first is called permanent insurance. The most common plan is whole life, which simply means you pay for the whole of your life. You pay from the time you start the policy until you die.

Whole life was very common at first, but some people years ago decided they would like to pay their life insurance policy up in a shorter period of time. Especially, they wanted to avoid paying premiums in their retirement years. So they would buy what is called *limited pay life*: most commonly a 20-pay life insurance plan. There are variables of course—there is 30-pay life and paid-up-at-65 life. But generally speaking, instead of paying the whole of your life you pay for a limited period of time.

In recent years, a product has emerged called Single Premium Life. With this product, you pay a single premium and it covers the insured for their entire life. As you can well imagine, if you are paying a whole life premium of x dollars, a 20-pay life would obviously require a larger premium–because you are spreading the payments out over 20 years. A Single Premium Life requires one large premium. We will explore this in more detail later on.

The second form of life insurance is called term insurance. The name includes the word "term" because this product provides coverage for a limited term period. Because it provides insurance for only a term –commonly 10 or 20 years–term insurance is much lower in cost than whole life insurance. Moreover, term insurance seldom develops any cash surrender values, which helps keep the cost of term insurance quite low.

Term insurance is a very valuable product in any agent's portfolio because of its low cost. Later in this book we will see examples where term insurance can be used quite a bit. For instance, it is excellent for young families who need a lot of life insurance but have a limited ability to pay.

By the way, most term insurance is *convertible*. That does not mean the car top goes down. That means term insurance can be converted into a permanent life insurance policy with no proof of insurability. To simplify, imagine you own a 20-year term insurance plan. You have owned this plan for ten years now, and you realize that you want the insurance for the rest of your life. Because your insurance is convertible, prior to its expiration you can exchange it for a permanent plan.

Again, normally this is done without requiring any proof of insurability. Even if you have contracted a very serious or possibly fatal disease, you just sign a form and the company will issue the new life insurance policy. This option is written into the details of your term insurance policy. It is a very, very important aspect of a term insurance policy to keep in mind. That wraps up our brief explanation of common life insurance products.

Annuities are very different. In fact, I always used to think of an annuity as a life insurance policy in reverse. But to be more precise, an annuity is an accumulation account with a *guaranteed base interest rate*. In today's market, interest rates are low—especially in banks. However, an annuity will have a guaranteed interest rate, such as 2%. If the company is financially successful and their investments return better than expected, the company may even pay an embellished interest rate. In fact, I just got a call from a company this morning: their basic annuity's interest rate is 2%, but they are currently paying out 3%. Of course, that is 50% higher! With annuities, that is just the way things go. When the company makes more money, they usually pay a higher rate of interest.

So, while an annuity has a guaranteed minimum interest rate, it will commonly earn a higher interest rate. When you examine annuities, they can compare very well to a bank savings account. At the time of this writing, banks pay about 0.5% interest on typical savings accounts. Some banks will pay more than that, but they usually require a large deposit and a commitment to leave the money for of a period of time. For example, a certificate of deposit requires that you keep your money there for at least a year or two.

Annuities have a real advantage in that they grow tax free. This is critical. This is key. It is why many people use annuities in their IRAs. If an individual has been putting as much money as possible into their IRA, they can invest in an annuity and it will grow tax free—just like it grows tax free in their IRA. And there is no limitation to the amount of money that you can deposit into annuities.

When you purchase an annuity, you name a beneficiary. Assume you have a normal life expectancy of age 85. If you died prematurely at age 65, your beneficiary would receive that annuity. Whatever money you had put into the annuity would have grown over time, perhaps even doubled. It grows tax free during that entire time period, but—and that is a capital BUT—the annuity's beneficiary would be required to pay taxes on that growth. In other words: the annuity grows tax free, but ultimately that growth must be taxed.

The bright side is that there is an advantage to having the money grow tax free. If the beneficiary is in a lower tax bracket than the original purchaser, the tax rate will be lower for them.

Another feature is that an annuity can be paid out in the form of a *lifetime guaranteed income*. Imagine that you are now 65 years old, having accumulated quite a sum in your annuity. You will want to withdraw funds from the annuity on a monthly basis for the rest of your life, to complement your pension and Social Security income. The life insurance company will calculate—based on the guaranteed figures in the annuity—how much they will pay you monthly for the rest of your life.

Annuities have a few other features, which most agents should know. For instance, the life insurance company will pay you from the annuity for the rest of your life, but may also guarantee the payments for a specified number of years. If you took your first annuity payment and then were killed in an airplane accident, you would never receive the huge amount of money the company promised to pay you. But lo and behold, out of that huge amount of money, the company could make 10 years of payments to your beneficiary if you planned ahead.

That is basically what an annuity is. It is a deferral of taxation, and it can be converted into lifetime income. Many people invest their money in the stock market, but at retirement decide to switch to an annuity because they do not want market risks anymore. Annuities can eliminate that risk. That is what annuities are all about.

CHAPTER 2

SELL SOLUTIONS, NOT PRODUCTS

I have titled this chapter "Sell Solutions, Not Products." It is very, very important that you focus on the word "solutions" and realize what I am saying. Selling *solutions* is what we really do for a career.

If you take your car into a service center and they inform you that your brakes are completely worn out, what do you ask? You ask about the solution. And the fellow replies, "In this case, the solution is simple. You need new brake pads and you need the rotors turned. If we put the new brake pads on there and turn the rotors, your car will stop just like it did when it was brand new." That is the solution for bad brakes.

If no one ever died, life insurance would have never been invented. It would not be a needed solution! But since we do die, life insurance is a solution for the financial issues that can follow a death—especially a premature death. Keep in mind that life insurance can also be a solution for diverse situations other than death. This is because of the unique tax preference that life insurance enjoys. Every agent must understand this tax preference. I mentioned annuities in the last chapter. Well, this is better than an annuity! Imagine that you leave an annuity to your heir. You initially invest $50,000, which grows over time to $100,000. Your heir will be required to pay taxes on the $50,000 of growth.

Contrast that with a life insurance policy. If you invest the same $50,000 into a Single Premium Life insurance policy, the death benefit 20 years out might be $100,000 (just like the annuity). But in this case, your heir will receive the life insurance payment *with zero taxes.* That is a huge benefit. In future chapters, we will explore how this feature of life insurance policies can open up whole new markets of big prospects.

Life insurance is a powerful product because it is a great *solution* for people's problems. If you are a Policy Peddler, I hate to say this, but you are going to stay in the minor leagues. A Policy Peddler is someone who focuses on the product they have to sell, instead of the solutions the product can offer. Early in business, we are all taught to go out and sell a $10,000 or $20,000 policy to everyone we know. But merely selling policies without selling *solutions for felt needs* is not the way to grow as a life insurance agent. Instead, you want to be a Solution Provider.

Let me tell you the story of how I served as a Solution Provider in a very special case. Be warned: you will have to think outside the box a little bit.

I was referred to a gentleman by a certain fellow. The fellow called me on the phone and told me about how old the man was, that he was wealthy, and that he had a huge amount of life insurance—which meant he was a believer in life insurance. Most importantly, this gentleman needed another big chunk of life insurance.

Because his estate was so large with all his properties, he wanted life insurance money to be available at his death to pay the estate taxes. That way, none of the properties would have to be liquidated. That was very important to him, and rightly so—these properties produced a large stable return. He did not want to let those go, and neither did his wife or the kids.

The fellow who handed me the referral gave me the man's name, his phone number, and where he lived. It was a good hour's drive away from me in a small town.

Before he finished, the referrer said to me, "Oh, by the way, one last thing. You cannot use my name when you approach him." Now, when you are given a referral, the most important part is the referrer's name! That element opens the prospect up to you: "Oh yeah, I know John really well. I am glad he told you to give me a call." Using the referrer's name breaks barriers down and makes the sales conversation easier.

But this fellow said that I could not use his name. I naturally asked him why, and he replied, "Well, a few years ago I took another insurance agent like you to see this gentleman. This agent put everything into shape so it was easier for the family to understand—a very, very complex task because the man had many policies. Then he made recommendations on new policies to purchase.

"This gentleman was very, very bright. He was worth over fifty million dollars, so you know he had to be intelligent. He caught this insurance agent doing a sly trick. Basically, the agent was trying to rob Peter to pay Paul. He wanted the man to withdraw thousands of dollars out of some older insurance policies to buy a new policy—which, of course, would trigger a new commission for the agent.

"But this guy knew his business inside and out, and he did not like that at all. He felt he was being taken advantage of, and he threw both of us out. He said, 'I never want to see either of you again.' My name is mud to him and it will not help you out a bit. At least you know what this guy has: a big estate problem. You have to figure out some kind of sensible approach."

I finished writing down the prospect's information, and then the referrer hung up. I did not hesitate five seconds: I picked up the phone and called the prospect. But I had to bluff him. When I got him on the phone, I introduced myself and said, "I am a professional in the life insurance field. I cannot remember exactly who mentioned your name, but I understand that you have a substantial amount of life insurance, and you are interested in some kind of a policy audit to get everything organized." He said "Yeah," and I said, "Well, I am going to be in your town next week, probably close to noon—perhaps 11:00. Suppose I drop into your office and introduce myself, and we will chat for a few minutes and see if there is anything I can do." He said "Yeah, that will be fine."

The ice was broken. He gave me time to see him. He now knew my name.

Side note: whenever I give anybody my name like that, I always have them jot my telephone number down in case something comes up and they have to change the time of the meeting. I make that very clear, and I say it very slow. People really like to get a phone number, because it takes the hook out a little bit. It gives them a way out if they suddenly decide to cancel.

I am not worried about them taking that way out, though. In my whole career, I do not think I have ever lost an appointment because I gave someone that option. On the other hand, there have been occasions where we had to change the appointment time. That is when my phone number really came in handy.

In this particular case, the gentleman had a big estate tax problem. I had to deal with that in order to earn a shot at his business. For now, I am going to keep you in suspense about the outcome of this referral. But do not worry—we will return to the story later.

CHAPTER 3.

MATCH PRODUCTS TO MARKETS

In order to become a Solution Provider, you absolutely must match the products that you have for sale (your "solutions") to the targeted marketplace.

You need to discover your ideal market or markets. Strangely enough, I have never seen an insurance company host a meeting and bring in an expert to teach agents how to discover their market.

Why is discovering your market necessary? Well, there are a number of markets in the life insurance industry. Those markets do not fit every personality. For Ben Feldman–the great New York Life producer for decades targeted big business owners.

Once I had the opportunity to spend several days with Ben and his staff. One of his sons told me, "Roger, Dad had this idea from the very beginning. He told my brother and I, 'We have to develop 100 big corporate clients. When we reach that number, we never have to worry about business after that. Because 100 corporate clients divided by 50 weeks in a year (with 2 weeks off for vacation) means that we need to meet with two of them each week. And good corporate clients can buy more life insurance than a hundred personal clients can buy, every single year. That is our business.' He knew exactly the market he wanted to go after."

Personally, I have always been very comfortable in the professional market. When I was young in business, a huge dinner meeting for medical professionals was hosted at my country club. My wife and I were invited and were happy to attend. I lived in an area of Fort Lauderdale, Florida called "Doctors' Row." So almost everyone at the meeting was a doctor.

When the evening's speaker got up to the microphone, he noticed me in the crowd. He was a client of mine, and he began to chuckle a bit. He said, "Folks, we are all medical people here–except I see Roger Gertz. Our insurance man is here!" Of course, I appreciated him pointing me out. Then he said, "Roger, I hope the ceiling does not fall in on this group tonight because I think it would bankrupt your insurance company." Everyone laughed, because I had insured just about everyone in the room for a million dollars or more. His joke turned out to be a marketing boost for me. I never forgot that.

As you sell life insurance over the months and years, you will begin to discover your ideal market–if you pay attention. What do your best clients have in common? What are their industries? Whom do you speak with most easily? Answer these questions and you are close to discovering your market.

SECTION II.

PERSONAL GROWTH

CHAPTER 4.

BECOME UNIQUE

Become unique. Do something out-of-the-ordinary to set yourself ahead of the crowd.

Here is an example. Years ago, a super-successful friend invited me to Chicago to attend a cable-TV convention. I told him when my flight was going to arrive and he said, "I will pick you up at O'Hare airport. When you walk out the main door, I will be waiting for you. I will wave at you, and you can jump into my car."

I did not give it much thought. But when I got out of the airport and looked for my friend, there was a huge line of Checker cabs. Lo and behold, this friend was standing next to a cab. I just thought he was standing there waiting for me, but when I got near him he told me, "Jump in!" I replied, "What did you do, hire a cab?" And he said, "No, this is my car." So we got in this Checker cab, and he laughed and explained things to me. "I never have a parking problem with this vehicle. Chicago traffic is crazy, and this ride makes life a lot easier for me. I can park anywhere for a few minutes or longer with no problem!"

I could not believe it. He bought this used Checker cab for practically nothing. I mean, he could buy a used Checker for 5% of the price of a new Cadillac. On the other hand, his office was on the 44th floor of the John Hancock building in Chicago. His apartment was on the 96th floor. Both were extremely impressive. By the way, note that there was no auto traffic between his home and office. Just elevator traffic. So the only reason he had a vehicle was to go pick up people at the airport in that Checker cab!

Do you think that set him apart from the crowd? I will never forget that for as long as I live. He was so unique. This guy was so clever, and he made millions of dollars, but he thought way outside of the box.

Think about how you could become unique in your business. You might specialize in a product, or you might be just a little different than everyone else. This guy chose to differentiate himself with his Checker cab. Being unique is very, very important. If you can be unique—not necessarily crazy, but unique—you will stand out from the crowd.

CHAPTER 5.

EDUCATE YOURSELF

I do not care what business you are in, there is nothing more important than constantly educating yourself. There is just nothing more important than that.

I kid everyone and say, "Get some alphabet soup after your name. It really pays big dividends." In this business, you should work towards your CLU (Chartered Life Underwriter) or CFP (Certified Financial Planner). It not only impresses prospects, but also will grow your knowledge and skills.

These courses are not just to impress. The CLU is the doctorate degree of life insurance, and being a CLU will make a big, big difference. More important than having letters after my name were what the courses taught me and what sales vistas the degree opened up for me. As a Chartered Life Underwriter, I can sell life insurance in any state without taking a state license exam. So, if I want to sell a big policy to a guy in Oregon, no problem. I just get an Oregon non-resident license, and because I am a CLU there is no exam. Simple as that. I give them my credit card and pay the basic fee for the license. Done.

Aside from educational courses, you should focus on learning technology. Technology has taken over the world. In a few short years, most insurance will be sold through some form of technology. Recently I was on the phone with my brilliant young programmer. We are now putting the insurance software we create (more on that later) onto thumb drives. I carry a thumb drive around with me at all times. Whether I am at a party or a Starbucks or a friend's house, everyone has a computer. Demonstrating the value of an insurance policy is as simple as plugging in my thumb drive and launching the software.

One useful tech tool for your business success is the website *Join.Me*. I use this service while on the phone with a prospect, in order to share my computer screen with them. The website URL is just Join.Me, no dot-com or anything. Best of all, it is free! When I call a prospect, I ask them to hop on the internet. Ninety-nine percent of the people I call already have a computer in front of them, whether they are at their home or in their office.

Once they are online, I tell them to type Join.Me into the address bar. When they arrive at the Join.Me site, they are presented with two options: *Start Meeting* or *Join Meeting*. When they click "Join Meeting" the webpage asks them for a 9-digit code, which I have because I am hosting the meeting. Once they type the number in, they can instantly see my computer screen in real time.

What is the advantage here? The prospect is looking at my computer through their computer, and they are listening to me on the telephone. I own two of their senses: sight and hearing. Their eyes and their ears are both focused on my visual screen. This eliminates distractions and puts all the focus on what I am showing them.

You need to become educated about your business, the products you offer, and how to use them. Additionally, you should become as technologically savvy as you can, because everyone uses computers and smartphones and tablets these days. And the progress of technology is not lessening. It is just going to grow faster and faster. Remaining unfamiliar with newer technologies can really hurt you.

I own a company named VisCalc, which is short for Visual Calculations. We convert all of those boring ledger statements you show prospects into engaging color visuals. Besides being more interesting, graphics aid comprehension 10 times better than plain words and numbers. So the VisCalc tools we create can really improve your productivity.

I am going to introduce something here that we will discuss at length near the end of the book. One of the craziest aspects of technology is software development. People nowadays are calling the things they produce "apps," short for "applications," which is another word for "software." Today apps are being created by the thousands.

At VisCalc, we develop apps for insurance agents. Our software is all designed to enhance, augment, and strengthen the agent's ability to make a stellar offering. I use the software products we create to close prospects, keep records, enhance my income, increase my productivity, and have a better life. The tiny size of the thumb drive in my pocket belies its true power.

ASSOCIATE WITH SUCCESS

During my first year in business, I enrolled in a Chartered Life Underwriter program, taught by one of the greatest insurance experts in the business. Never did I miss a class–the content was pure gold. At that class in Fort Lauderdale, age 25, I met a very successful producer who changed my life. I was driving a two-door VW Bug, but he was driving a shiny new Cadillac convertible. I was dressed for business, but he was dressed for success. I wore a suit and tie, while he dressed for the type of prospect he was seeing that day.

He and I connected, and I joined his company. He was the Vice President of this company, but also a producer. He had made a deal with the company, and though he was the Vice President, he did not even have an office at the company–because he was never there. He made more money than all the company's executive staff combined, because he was a huge producer.

He got me licensed with his company, and showed me all the highlights of their products. As this relationship progressed, I asked him a question. "Bill, could I come to your office and ride around with you for a few days? I just want to observe your strategies and techniques."

His office is only about an hour from my home, so it was not an inconvenience. Plus it was in Florida, where the weather is nice all the time. The morning of the first day I asked, "Well, what are we going to do today?" He responded, "Well Roger, in about an hour we are going to go meet a fellow and deliver a policy. Then we have a lunch appointment at noon with an attorney that I want you to meet. It will be a long lunch, probably an hour and a half. Then I have another case with a new prospect, and that will be it for the day." That was definitely enough for a full day!

We got into his car and went to his ten o'clock appointment. I noticed he had brought no briefcase. He was just dressed well–dressed really sharp. I asked him, "So what are we going to do again?" He reached into the vest pocket of his sport coat and pulled out a policy. He handed it to me and replied, "We are going to deliver this policy. Take a look." Opening the policy, I saw in astonishment that it was for a million dollars. I knew what my commission rate was, and my commission on that million-dollar policy would be nearly $50,000. His commission rate was higher than mine! In those days I never earned $50,000 in an entire year. He was about to deliver that policy and make $50,000 in one shot!

Needless to say, I was glad to be riding along with him. I wanted to see what he did! We arrived at this fellow's workplace and entered. We were shown into his very nice office–he was obviously wealthy enough to pay the huge policy premium. Bill introduced me to the man (we will call him Mr. Smith) then asked, "Would you mind if Roger sat in on our conversation? He is one of my new representatives." Mr. Smith said, "No, that is fine. Roger, good to get to know you."

Bill sat directly across from the prospect, and I sat alongside them on a sofa. Bill started the conversation by asking, "Did you enjoy talking with Dr. Black?"

"Well, needless to say, yes, I really enjoyed it. And wow is he knowledgeable!"

"Oh yes he is. Dr. Black teaches Law and Estate Planning at the University of Florida. When it comes to estate planning, he is the number one teacher in the state."

Bill, I cannot thank you enough for introducing me to Dr. Black."

"You are very welcome. So, Mr. Smith, how was your conversation with him?"

"Well, Bill, frankly it was several conversations. Dr. Black called and introduced himself just like you said he would. He set up a time when we could talk, and I gave him a lot of information. After he had gathered everything he needed to know, he told me that he might have to call back for a few details, but he wanted to put something together. He called back a week later and we talked through his suggestions.

"And it turns out you were right. Dr. Black said that the best way for me to fund my estate tax liability is through life insurance, because I am a real estate developer."

Bill reached into his vest pocket, pulled out the policy, handed it to Mr. Smith, and said, "This is what Dr. Black says you need."

The man looked at the policy for a bit, then said, "Right here on the front of the policy, it looks like the premium is nearly $50,000. Is that correct?"

"Yes, that is correct."

"Well, that is a pretty big bite out of my bank account, Bill."

"Yes, it does appear to be a big bite. But let me show you something. Open the policy to page 13."

Mr. Smith opened the policy to page 13, which was the policy's cash value table. Bill said, "You see in the left-hand column years one through twenty. In the next column is the cash value of the policy, which you will notice starts out in year one with not much at all. However, the cash value increase in the second year is almost $50,000. So this is not a $50,000 cost–it is a $50,000 *transfer payment*.

"See, all you do is go down to the bank and transfer that amount into this policy. Your money in the policy will grow the same rate as it would if it were sitting in the bank."

The man responded, "Yeah, I can see that. Except for that first year–I take a pretty good-sized hit that year."

"That is true. The reason is that the company has expenses: medical reports, exams, commissions, set up fees... the cost of doing business. They roll all of those expenses into the first year's cost."

Mr. Smith said, "Well, that is still a pretty large hit."

"Is that the only thing that bothers you?"

"Frankly, yes."

Bill looked at Mr. Smith and asked, "Do you still own that home in Boca Raton, Florida on Rio Vista that is been for sale now for over a year?"

"Yes I do. How did you know about that?"

"Well, when I talked with Dr. Black he told me you had some property that had not sold for over a year. You were kind of tired of it, but the property would not sell.

So I called a good friend of mine who is a real estate agent. I asked him to take a look at the house and tell me how much he thinks it is worth. After talking to him, we are pretty sure the house is worth somewhere near $50,000."

(Remember that this was years ago–the sum would be closer to a million dollars today.)

Mr. Smith responded, "Yes, that sounds about right."

"Okay then. Deed the house to me and I will pay the $50,000 premium for you. We both win!"

"Are you serious?"

"Absolutely. Here is my attorney's card. Just have your attorney call him and set up a closing. When I leave here, I will overnight a $50,000 check to the company to pay the policy premium."

Mr. Smith stuck out his hand and said, "You have yourself a deal there, buddy."

"Excellent. Glad I could help you out."

Everyone was happy as we walked out. As we got into his beautiful Cadillac convertible I said, "Oh my goodness, Bill. You just made $50,000. And you never had a sales interview with this guy! You only had a delivery interview."

"Roger, we are a few miles from Palm Beach. These folks are the wealthiest people in the United States. I am not going to try to sell them on a bunch of detail. I introduce them to Dr. Black, the finest estate planner in the state of Florida. He does the set up. I just do the delivery."

I closed my eyes and repeated, "Oh my goodness. Bill, I cannot believe what I just saw."

He replied, "Selling this insurance is really easy *when you match your product to the market.*"

I travelled with Bill on several more appointments. If I told you the name of some of his clients, you would not believe me. Their names are well-known in the United States. Bill just had the guts and the wherewithal to go after that level of business. He made it look so easy.

But what if you do not have that kind of gumption?

That is okay. You do not have to live in Palm Beach and go after multimillionaires to successfully apply the strategies in this chapter.

Let me tell you another tale, and then I will explain the moral of both stories.

A few weeks later, I had an appointment with a fellow who owned an elevator company. He installed small elevators for multi-floor condos and the like. My parents knew him well—name of Harold Smith, really a nice guy. His friends called him "Smitty".

I visited Harold because he needed some life insurance. Now, the policy I got for him was not a million-dollar policy like the one Bill sold. It was a quarter-million-dollar policy. But it still had a pretty sizable premium.

Walking into Harold's office for the delivery appointment, I noticed a brand new red Mustang sitting in his reserved parking spot. This model had just come out, and it was a good-looking car. Seated in his office, I said, "Well Smitty, it looks like you got yourself a new sports car out there."

"Actually no. Roger, that is my son's car, and I am so mad I could kill that kid."

"What is the matter?"

"I got him that car for his 16th birthday. Dumbest thing I ever did. That was only a month ago, and he has already received three speeding tickets! The car is sitting there because I guess I am taking it away from him."

"Oh. Looks like you are stuck with a Mustang."

"Yeah."

I knew approximately what that Mustang cost, and though I cannot remember the price exactly it must have been a few thousand dollars in those days.

We carried on with the policy delivery appointment, and it reminded me of the big million-dollar situation I was in with Bill. Harold looked at the policy and said, "That is a pretty good-sized premium." I told him to look at page 13: think of it as a transfer payment. The same way Bill had presented it.

Harold still was not sure.

Now remember–I was driving a fabulously good-looking VW Bug (sarcasm alert). My million-dollar-policy-delivering friend Bill had a gorgeous convertible Cadillac, and I was still driving a VW Bug.

"Smitty, I have a good idea."

"What is that?"

I reached into my pocket and pulled out the keys to my VW.

"You know I am driving that VW out there. Since you are mad at your son, here is an idea for you. I will give you my VW, and you will give me the Mustang. In return, I will pay for the policy. You give your kid the VW, and that will teach him a good lesson."

"You have a deal there, Roger. You have a deal there. That is the best idea I have heard all week."

So just a few weeks after I met Bill with his Cadillac, I moved up to a Mustang. By applying the same technique Bill used, I rid myself of the VW and got a brand new sports car.

The moral of the story:

Think outside the box.

And how do you move your thinking there?

Associate with successful people who are already fantastic outside-the-box thinkers.

When you see a successful agent use an amazing strategy or technique, you will never forget it. You just cannot. The strategy is so different that it makes an enduring impression on you. You learn how to use these methods. Thinking over my long career, I can recall many crazy things that have occurred because of outside-the-box on-the-spot thinking. But if you have never seen it in action, you do not know how it works. You need to observe others.

You do not have to be the world's best salesperson. You just have to have an arsenal of tools—an outside-the-box toolbox. You get those tools by watching them in use.

And you do not have to go after million-dollar policy sales. Or even quarter-million-dollar policy sales! You can apply these techniques to a CPA you know, or a high-powered local attorney. Once you learn the strategies, you can use them in any market.

Learn how to think outside the box of your own mind. Try to think *inside* the prospect's mind. What is on his mind? If you can figure that out, you are halfway to a great solution and a sale.

Harold had a son with a new Mustang. He did not want to return the Mustang to the dealership. But he did not want to let his boy keep driving it. So I provided Harold with a solution. He was happy to hand the VW keys to his son and say, "You are going to drive this for the next few years until you graduate. We will see if you can drive for a couple years without a speeding ticket, and then we will talk about getting you another Mustang."

Harold was happy.

I was happy.

And it all came about because I chose to associate myself with a successful peer like Bill.

SECTION III.

THE PROSPECT PROCESS

CHAPTER 7.

ANALYZE YOUR PROSPECTS

I opened this book up with a comment by Jesse James. Supposedly, a sheriff asked Jesse, "Why do you rob banks?" Jesse replied, "Because that is where the money is." A smart-aleck response, but one that reveals a profound truth. If you are selling insurance and annuities, you want to sell *where the money is*. You want to sell to people who actually have the money to buy! At the top of my list are doctors, lawyers, business owners, company officers, retired wealthy individuals, the millionaire next door, and anyone else you know who is particularly well off.

Years and years ago, I had a good friend who mailed out a weekly stock market letter to several thousand subscribers. He wrote a four-page newsletter, very in-depth and well done. During the week he would gather up information about the stock market—whether it had gone up or down or sideways or whatever it does. At the end of the week he wrote the letter very quickly. On Saturday he would print the letter at his own print shop and have it mailed out, ready to arrive in his subscribers' mailboxes on Monday.

Talking to him about this issue, of who has the money to buy life insurance, I asked him: "Do you have any ideas on how to construct a direct mail letter?" This guy was a little older than me, but he was incredibly bright. A few days after I asked him that question, he showed up at my house and rang the doorbell. When I opened the door he was standing there with his thick glasses and a notebook. I said, "Hey Don, how are you doing?" He replied, "Roger, I want to read you this direct mail letter that I wrote for you." When he read me the letter, I could not believe how simple, direct, and powerful it was.

He said to me, "Roger, I have the printing and mailing facilities. My printing presses are only real busy on Saturday when I print my newsletter. If you want, I know where to buy the direct mail list we need. We will print up this letter, and I suggest we send the first round of letters to doctors and lawyers because that is an easy mailing list to buy."

This was years ago when postage was very inexpensive. The letter was delivered in a number ten envelope—the address appeared through the window in the envelope, and it seemed official. It looked like one of those "I-had-better-open-this letters, because it might be official, or there might be money in it." The envelope screamed, "Open me, open me, open me!"

The letter generated a hard-core 1% response. Now that is not very high, but remember what I said: it was a *hard-core* 1% response. We had mailed out about 5,000 letters, so I had about fifty responses. At that time I had a pretty good-sized insurance agency, so I called an agency meeting with a dozen agents. I showed them all the direct mail letter that we mailed out. I showed them the responses. They knew all about the policy and what to sell. I told them, "Fellas, make sure you make all of these calls this week and go on as many appointments as possible. Next week at the agency meeting, I am going to ask all of you to give a report as to how it turned out and what happened."

Now comes the rest of the story.

At the next weekly meeting I could not believe the response. *Almost none of the agents called on any of the direct mail respondents.* Needless to say, I was absolutely furious. I do not get mad very easily, but at that point I said, "Gentlemen, I want you to turn in your prospect lead cards to the secretary, because you had a week to call them and you did not. I want them back." By that evening my secretary had all the lead cards back. She asked me, "What do you want me to do with them, Roger?" I said, "Give them to me."

I was fuming I was so mad. The next day I had all those cards in front of me and I got on the telephone. I had *the biggest day I ever had* in my life insurance career. Maybe not the biggest commission day, but the biggest appointment day. I had set two breakfast appointments, a mid-morning appointment, two lunch appointments, and a later-afternoon appointment. Six life insurance interviews in one day! It was probably a world record. These were six honest-to-goodness appointments with people that I had never met, but I made telephone appointments with every one of them.

You know what I came back with at the end of that sales day? I came home with *seven completed applications*, and almost every policy was for $100,000 or greater. I only saw six people, but I had seven applications, because one fellow bought a $50,000 policy on his wife. So I had the biggest and most successful day in my life insurance career from an appointment standpoint.

Plus, this was many years ago, back when an agent who made $25,000 annually was rolling in the dough. That one day, my commissions were over $12,000 from those sales.

How do you think the next agency meeting went?

Okay, just to drive the point home, here is another story that is almost as ridiculous as the first. Once an insurance agent, who was not in my agency but was a good friend of mine, happened to be in my office. He saw my pile of direct mail cards, which were simply 3x5 IBM cards. People would just write their name and date of birth on the card and then send it back in the mail, postage paid. We paid the postage when we received the card.

My friend saw the pile and asked me, "What are those?" I told him that I had a direct mail campaign going, and these were the people who had responded. He glanced at the top card on the pile, and lo and behold it was an attorney friend of his from church. Since I was feeling generous, I decided to give him the lead card. It probably cost me $15 for the lead, but I just handed it to him since he was a friend. I said, "Okay. Here is the policy rate card and here is the application. Call the attorney and sell it to him. If you sell him, you can buy me lunch."

A week later I saw my friend again. I asked him, "How did you do with that lead I gave you?" His head dropped and he reached into his vest pocket. He pulled out the response card and said, "I have not called him yet."

This was a couple weeks after the original agency meeting. So what do you think happened? I got the same boil inside as before, and I took the reply card back. I told him, "I am sorry you did not call, but I am going to take this lead back because you did not move on it. Leads have a half-life: the longer they sit around, the less they are worth."

Later the same day I called that prospect. I cannot use his name now because his name is a household word in the United States. If I said his name, you would associate it with his very wealthy family. To make a long story short, I called him up, saw him the next day, and sold him my first million-dollar policy.

A month or so later, the same agent who did not make the phone call was in my office again. He looked down at the stack of mail on my desk, and there laid a window envelope with a check from the insurance company that wrote the million-dollar policy. I opened the envelope, pulled out the check, and showed it to him. "This is what you gave me, because you did not call that lead." The check was for over $15,000–it would be worth more like $40,000 today.

My friend learned from that experience, and was always quicker to call the leads he received.

What should we learn from these two stories? First, always contact your leads quickly. Second, and more to the point for this chapter, *it is profitable to target people who can pay*. That is why I say you should analyze your prospects. We only sent the direct mail to doctors and lawyers, so everyone who received the letter could afford the product. When I picked up the phone to call one of the respondents, I was not thinking, “Oh I hope he can afford it.” I knew better.

CHAPTER 8.

HOW TO MEET PEOPLE

Stop making cold calls.

Cold calls create an "icy" sales climate. You want to speak warmly to referrals. Cold calls are just tough, and the environment is cold. Once in a while a cold call will work out great—but the others, not so much. In the prospect's mind, you are a stranger. You must do everything right. You must look the part, talk the part and act the part. Everything must work out perfectly if a cold call is to pay off. Transitioning to work with warm leads and referrals will change your entire career.

When you find a warm prospect, go for the soft sell. Do not go hard. Use phrasing like, "When might it be convenient to talk?" That question does not push them to make a decision immediately. Take the pressure off with something light.

Now you just need to find a bunch of warm prospects. What are the best situations to do this? Well, there are many.

If you are with a fraternal life insurance company, they host a lot of fraternal events. Many of these are social meetings, like picnics or sports events, because fraternal life insurance companies are kind of like family. Attend these meetings!

Speaking of family, family gatherings are great. You go to a family gathering, there is bound to be some new friend of the family attending. Early in my career, I realized that parties and sporting events are great places to meet people. So are coffee shops where people sit around casually. I love experiencing these situations, where I can meet people who might qualify and need what I am selling. People in these circumstances are under the least pressure for time and money, and thus are more open to talking.

When you are in the company of people you know very little about, *you must listen and ask questions*. You do not learn anything by telling a prospect who you are and what you do. You need to listen. Correctly sizing up the prospect is essential.

You should be equipped to hand them your business card if they ask for it. I always ask people for their business cards, and when they hand it to me I do not just stick it in my pocket. I look at it, because I want to know what they do. When I look at the business card it often triggers the next conversation topic. For instance, they might be the VP or in a high position, or the company might be extra-large or unique. Whatever I can see on the business card will trigger my next step, inquiring about their business.

If you are in a more casual situation, you might ask them about their family. You want to build rapport with people, genuinely make a friend out of them. Some salespeople think this sounds crazy, but remember: sales are not made quickly. A Policy Peddler might go out and sell a $10,000 policy really quick, but you do not want to be a Policy Peddler. If you focus on building an authentic friendship the first time around, you will discover that your relationship is on a much higher level the second time you meet.

If you are comfortable speaking in public, offer to speak to groups. Even if your topic of choice is not life insurance per se, you can include comments about it that will appeal to some audience members. For instance, fraternal insurance agencies host fraternal meetings every month or every quarter. The groups vary in size from a dozen people to perhaps forty. The event might be a picnic, a trip, or a sporting event like bowling. If you have opportunity to speak to such a group, you can tailor your speech with enough information to draw questions from the audience.

In fact, you should always ask for questions. Whenever I speak to a group, I start off differently than most: "Before I address you on this topic, there is a ground rule I want to establish."

That sounds kind of rude, cruel, and harsh. The whole room is quiet. I continue: "I love interruptions!" Everyone laughs and is put at ease. "If you have a question, raise your hand and I will be happy to answer it. Some folks are uncomfortable with interrupting a speaker, so you might jot a question down for me to address during the question-and-answer period. Does that sound okay to everyone?"

This approach works like magic. As a speaker, I am no longer on my podium in an aloof position. I become part of the group. People talk to me as part of the group. The effect is absolutely magical.

If you do not have enough prospects to call, start thinking. Think of ways to get in front of new people. Obvious places include Chamber of Commerce meetings, business networking groups, church men's or women's groups, and on and on.

Kids who play sports open up doors for conversations. Boy, I sure spent a lot of afternoons and evenings at sporting events. And all the other kids' parents are there too! What a great opportunity to meet new people. In fact, children's events of any kind–Boy Scouts, youth retreats, class get-togethers–can be fantastic.

Ever heard of a "tag-along lunch"? No? That is because I made them up. But after you learn about them, you should definitely start doing tag-along lunches! When I do not have anything particularly urgent to do near lunchtime, and my wife is having lunch with someone, I might just tag along. Meeting my wife's friends, I cannot tell you how valuable those conversations have been. My wife is socially adept, so she gets in front of more important people than I ever could. I was fortunate to marry a lovely woman who has always been a real asset to me.

Volunteer projects are another opportunity to meet people and spent a lot of time talking. A group at my church decided to paint the house of a lady who lived down the street. We all pitched in a few dollars and bought the paint, then went to work. It took a whole Saturday, but I got to spend hours with my project coworkers. Result: Two nice-sized sales.

Prospects are everywhere. Be friendly, meet people, and look for opportunities to help solve genuine needs.

CHAPTER 9.

THREE PRINCIPLES FOR SOCIAL SUCCESS

While prospecting, you will find yourself in many neat social situations. It might be a family reunion, a church get-together, or a Super Bowl party. Regardless of the specific circumstances, common principles govern how you should relate in social situations. So here for your reading pleasure are my "*Three Principles for Social Success*".

Principle 1. Ask Light Questions

In a social situation, I suggest that you ask a lot of lightweight questions. For instance, to someone you just met: "What kind of business are you involved in?" Then wait and listen for the answer. If their business is foreign to you or particularly unique, you might follow with something like, "What does your product do for your customers?" Or, "I would sure like to visit your business sometime and see how you make those widgets."

Principle 2. Be Curious

In his fantastic book *How to Win Friends and Influence People*, Dale Carnegie shares six ways to make people like you. Number four is particularly appropriate here: "Be a good listener. Encourage others to talk about themselves."

Be curious about other people. Ask a question, then listen—really listen. Dig deeper. If they lighten up and appear to like talking about their self, this is always an open door. When an individual perks up and begins talking about himself, it is vital that you move along at a slow, reserved speed.

Above all, when another person is talking about himself, never interrupt to talk about *yourself*! The fifth of Stephen Covey's *7 Habits of Highly Effective People* is "Seek first to understand, then to be understood." Covey speaks of our tendency to respond to others *autobiographically*. That is, we start talking about ourselves. This shuts down lines of communication and alienates all involved. Instead, be curious about the other person. Focus on them and ask good questions: key, but still subtle questions.

Principle 3. Remember

Remember what others say to you. I suggest that you note your answers on something, even if it is your smartphone. As I always say, "Smartphones are for smart people to make smart moves." Taking notes so you can remember what someone said is definitely a smart move.

Ask for their business card, and always carry cards with you in case they ask you for your card. They may not, but you should be ready. Remember the old Boy Scout motto: Be Prepared!

After I finish conversing with someone, I might walk into a restroom or someplace quiet and use the space to take down a note or two. It sounds kind of weird, but I do not want to forget anything important. I do not want to forget people. I want to remember names; I want to remember businesses; I want to remember the key information they shared.

It is neat to ask someone for their opinion, and then remember their opinion through your notes. When you see the prospect a second time–which might be weeks or months later–ask something about himself or his business that you remember from your first encounter. This will totally set you apart from everyone else. People are more attracted to people who care about them than people who are just trying to sell them. Attraction first, sales come later.

To wrap up this chapter, let me mention three key tips.

1. Read Dale Carnegie's book *How to Win Friends and Influence People*. It has been around for years and years, with good reason. That little book has probably changed the lives of more salespeople than any other book. Dale Carnegie delivers wonderful insights on how to turn strangers into friends and influence others successfully. After all, that what selling is made up of.

2. Here is a newer idea. Nowadays we all carry cell phones with cameras in them. Taking pictures with others has become a common activity. Some people threw me a surprise birthday party at Starbucks recently, and I had more "selfies" taken with other people than you can imagine. Getting into a photo with others is not intimidating anymore. Years ago you had to pose and stand still for a while. Now you just stand up and smile, tap the smartphone's screen, and you have yourself a picture.

   If you have connected well with someone, grab a photo together before you leave. It will solidify the connection and help you remember their face in addition to their name.

3. When you read a good newspaper or magazine articles, ask yourself, "Who else might enjoy this?" If you have a prospect who might enjoy the article and find it helpful, make a copy of the article or send them an email. Say, "Hey Charlie, I read this great article in such-and-such a magazine, and I thought of you, and I thought you might like a copy. It might be of interest to you." That is only a little thing, but you have absolutely nothing to lose. And everything to gain.

CHAPTER 10.

PRACTICE FIRST ON THE WORST

We agents have been taught from day one to have a prospect list. The methods of accomplishing this are manifold. Some people keep a physical list on 3x5 cards or in their notebook; others make their list on the computer. You make notes about each person: where you met them, what you talked about, their occupation, their interests, special needs. Your list will remind you of important details when you call the prospect on the telephone. This prevents you from looking like a dummy, and puts you out ahead of the crowd.

Whether physical or electronic, your list should contain an aspect of *ranking*. You need to know who your best and worst prospects are. By *best* and *worst* I do not mean that the people themselves are good or bad. Instead, these terms refer to the prospects' ability to buy your product.

Once you have ranked your prospects, *practice first on the worst.* After rating people based on their value and their ability to buy, start presenting to the least-likely prospects. Since you are trying new strategies and growing in your presentation ability, using up the worst prospects first is sensible. If you mess up, your loss is not devastating.

But do not keep hanging around the bottom of the barrel. Go after some of the big sales opportunities too. Once you have practiced on the lower-rated leads, go after the top prospects. You practice so you can succeed in the "big game." Do not stay at practice sessions and miss the big game.

Open up your prospect list every day. Keep the sales process flowing. On any day you have not taken action to develop more sales, you might as well be on vacation or playing golf. You are not moving the business forward!

Roy H. Williams is a bestselling author and marketing expert who lives in Austin, Texas. He says,

"Unrelenting action is what turns starry-eyed daydreams into steely-eyed objectives.

You say you have a goal.

Let me look into your eyes.

Now tell me what you are going to do today."

If your goal is to gain more business, what are you going to do about it? Take action today.

Imagine that you have met three new people earlier today at a social event. Add them to your prospect list and rank them. Then schedule appointments with all three, leaving the best for last. Maybe your Thursday appointment is with a high-powered attorney, and your Tuesday appointments are with the less-likely prospects. Use the Tuesday appointments to practice for the Thursday appointment. Of course, you want to sell them all. But if all you get out of the first two appointments is practice, you will not be too disappointed.

Here is a personal story of how I practiced first on the worst. When I lived in Northwestern Ohio, I was a member of the local Chamber of Commerce. It was a good Chamber, with members from businesses of all different sizes. I attended the meetings semi-regularly.

One day, the Vice President of a large tire company called me. He told me, "Roger, I need some help. I am the Membership Chairman for the Chamber of Commerce this year."

I knew what was coming. He was going to ask me to be on his membership team. Glancing at my calendar, I started trying to figure out how to escape this deal. What a mistake that would have been!

Since the man was a church friend, I could not fib my way out. I just asked, "Okay. what is my responsibility?"

"Roger, it is very simple. You show up on Monday morning and have breakfast with the Membership Committee. We will go through the entire Chamber presentation, laying out why a business should join the Chamber. We have membership packets put together already. At the end of breakfast, you take five 3X5 lead cards with you and contact the people on those cards. Throughout the week, your job is to make as many personal appointments with these five people as possible and try to sell them the Chamber membership."

I agreed to help him out and met with the team that Monday. The next Friday evening, the Chamber hosted a party and a dinner for all the Chamber membership drive members. Quite a few people attended. My friend–we will call him Charlie–came over to me and said hello. I said hello back then asked him, "Where do I turn in these membership forms and checks and everything?" He then asked, "How did you do?"

"I did just what you said. I showed up Monday at the meeting, and I took five packets with five lead cards. I called all five people. Made all five appointments. Sold all five of them. Got five signed membership forms. Got five checks."

"You mean to tell me you sold every one of them?!?"

"Yeah. Was I not supposed to?"

Charlie was holding the microphone. He turned it on and announced to all 100 people in the room:

"Listen up everybody, listen up everybody. For the first time in the history of the Chamber of Commerce, one of our membership team–Roger Gertz–sold all five of his membership prospects. This is the first time in the history of the Chamber of Commerce that this has ever been done."

Everybody clapped. I was very pleased, since he had just given me quite a compliment.

During dinner, they presented all of the results of the Chamber membership drive. Then it was Charlie's turn at the microphone again. He said, "I am going to do something different. I am going to ask Roger Gertz to come up here and explain how he sold all five of his membership contacts."

Walking up to the microphone, I kept asking myself, *what am I going to say? What am I going to say?* I was not really comfortable telling them what I did, so I said something very different. I took the microphone and started off:

"Folks, if I told you how I closed 100% of my leads and picked up the forms and the checks from every one of them, I would have to have the doors locked and bolted. And I am sorry to say, I would have to kill all of you."

Everyone stared at me, astounded looks on their faces.

Laughing, I continued: "I cannot release my trade secret as a salesman. But,"—looking at the Chamber President, who was seated at the head table—"I will tell *you*. On one condition. You buy me breakfast here again next Monday morning, and I will share with you how to double your Chamber membership this year."

He replied, "Roger, you are on."

What was my secret?

I took my software.

I had developed two amazing software programs for small businesses. At the membership appointments, I explained my software and made it a gift if they became members of the Chamber. They could not turn me down.

Upon my explaining this to the Chamber president, he got so excited that we went straight across to the Chamber building and set up my software programs. We used the two programs (more on them later) to create the Chamber's employee handbook and the Chamber's employee benefits statements—all without the usual hassle and large expense.

During the next year, the Chamber referred me to business on which my agency earned over $250,000 in commissions.

All this came about because I made five presentations to my "worst" prospects. They were likely not going to buy. Since I had nothing to lose, I brought the software and incorporated it into my presentation. In the end, these five deals turned out to be my best move of the decade.

You just never know. I write this with a smile on my face—you just never know. That is why you have to practice on the worst—you will make discoveries you never would have otherwise. You never know where the "worst" prospects will really rank. You might be surprised. In fact, you should count on it.

CHAPTER 11.

USE THE RIGHT SALES EQUIPMENT

Most life insurance agents carry a briefcase and a laptop to interviews.

I think this is dead wrong.

My advice: Leave your briefcase and computer at home.

You are probably thinking, "Great. I have left all my stuff at home. How can I make a life insurance presentation and write some business without my equipment?"

I will answer that question, but first, just think about it for a minute. A briefcase can be intimidating. It might not look intimidating to you, but to some people it is. Besides, you might as well be wearing a t-shirt with large neon letters spelling out, "I AM A SALESPERSON. PREPARE TO GET SOLD!"

Do not carry a briefcase to the first interview if you can avoid it. Usually, you can store the necessary information in your head. If you need to take notes, bring some 3X5 cards or use a recording app on your smartphone. The point: In the first meeting, do not look like a salesperson.

If you absolutely positively need more equipment than that, borrow the prospect's equipment.

You ask, "How do I do that?"

I will tell you. Here is an example I fondly refer to as... The Super Bowl Story. A number of years ago, a number of guys decided to get together and watch the Super Bowl. During the game, we got into some conversations about life insurance. So what did I say? "We should turn the Super Bowl off, and I will get my computer out of the car to show you life insurance stuff"? Of course not! That would be ridiculous.

The party's host—a guy named Bert—seemed to be the most interested. So I stayed after the Super Bowl ended. As everyone else was walking out, I glanced around and saw Bert's computer sitting in his study. I said to him, "Bert, do you have just one minute? I would like to show you something. But I need to use your computer."

He said that was fine, so we walked into his study and sat down in front of the computer. I pulled out a memory stick from my pocket and plugged it in. That memory stick contains all the software programs I use to explain and sell life insurance.

I opened up the right program and started showing things to Bert. Since we had just talked about this during the Super Bowl, Bert was already interested. He became more interested as our conversation progressed. After half an hour Bert said to me, "Man, I need to do this."

I replied, "Well, since we have been here 30 minutes, how about we do 5 minutes more?"

"What do you mean?

"Let me show you." My memory stick also holds all the life insurance forms I might need, so I opened one and printed it using the printer sitting next to his computer. "Since I am here already, filling out this form will only take us 5 minutes. We should do it now."

It was a million-dollar sale.

It was a million-dollar sale, and I did not use any traditional sales equipment at all. I used the prospect's equipment.

In today's computer age—with crazy cell phones and smart watches and more—sales equipment is being transformed. Oh, I use sales equipment, but I hide it.

You do not want to look like a salesman. You want to look like an advisor. You want to look like a friend.

When you visit your doctor, he does not carry a big briefcase. He might have a notepad and jot down notes as you are talking. You can take the same approach. If you do not feel confident making the sale without your equipment, use the first meeting just to gather information. Then say, "We can get back together next week. I will do some research and bring you a solution."

Next meeting, you can bring your briefcase and computer. The prospect will be expecting it. And you will seem more like a doctor than a salesperson, because of how you handled your sales equipment.

CHAPTER 12.

BE PATIENT

When you meet someone and think they are a hot prospect, be patient. You do not have to close the sale the first time you meet someone. You are setting up a future meeting.

My son is an expert at this. He listens because he truly wants to learn about people. He does not mind going to a second interview; plus, the deals are of such significance that they are probably going to take multiple meetings anyway.

The old adage says that the early bird gets the worm. And that is true. The early bird gets the worm, but that does not mean he eats the whole worm that same morning. It just means he got the worm before any other bird.

The same with you: be the "early bird" by connecting with the prospect first. You can close the deal later on.

Gather data at the first appointment, but do not begin selling prematurely. Otherwise you will come across like a salesman. You should be slow to move, because you do not want the prospect to get the impression that that you are only concerned about yourself and your sale.

Before the advent of the smartphone, I carried a little tiny recording device, which was the size of a thick cell phone. After the lunch, meeting, or social gathering, I would quickly record everything I could remember about the person. Their business card would come in handy here. I would say, "Charlie is the vice president of *so-and-so*, and he has a really good job, and they do *this*, and he mentioned *that*." Later I would look over the data and ponder the information I had gathered. Many times I would go talk to an associate about the prospect. We were in an agency together, and we stayed friendly and worked together. Sometimes an associate will share an insight you never would have come up with on your own. Do not forget to go online and check out the prospect's website.

If you are unsure about anything, get counsel. Remember: you do not have to close the sale immediately. You do not have to move fast on the sale, because fast is often ineffective. You only want to propose a solution once you are fully prepared to do so. Additionally, consider rehearsing your strategy with an associate or your sales manager.

Let me share an example. One of the agents who reported to me was named Gary; he is still a good friend of mine. Gary is a very friendly, easy-to-meet fellow. One day he came into my office and said, "Roger, I met somebody and I want to run some ideas past you. If you do not mind, I really need your help on this."

Gary had gathered information well. This prospect and his wife were wealthy, and were both open to insurance. The wife was in good health, but the husband was not. They had a significant amount of money in their bank accounts.

After he finished sharing this valuable information, Gary asked me, "Roger, would you mind going on the interview with me? At least the initial interview?" I was his manager, so of course I said that I would not mind. Their home was not that far away from our office anyway. I told him to set up the appointment and let me know when it was scheduled.

At the appointment, Gary did not try to push the sale. He just said, "This is Roger Gertz, my manager. You mentioned some things when we talked the other day, and I just felt more comfortable bringing Roger along because he has been in the business longer." The guy said that he appreciated that, and we began a friendly conversation.

With that introduction, Gary handed the ball to me. The door was open for me to gather data, and I did that, but I did not try to close him. At the end of the meeting I said, "I would like to take a few days to look these details over. I will put something together, and since we are getting computerized, I will put it in a report format for you. You can look it over, and then you can see if we are heading in the right direction." I was very, very light on him. I was not pushy at all.

Gary gave the prospect the report. When he returned to the office, he told me that the prospect was really impressed. A few days later Gary and I went back for the last meeting, and the sale was simple because we had not been pushy. We gathered data and pondered it for a few days, and that made us professionals. A policy pusher would never have been able to make that sale.

Well, the bottom line is that this prospect put $600,000 into a single premium life insurance policy. We made him a lot of money, and he sent Gary lots of leads because our approach was so different. We were not policy peddlers. We were unique.

CHAPTER 13

HOW TO HANDLE CHINA EGGS

China Egg (noun): A big prospect you are afraid to call on, because you might screw up the deal or blow the sales interview.

Like a real egg made out of china, you are afraid to handle any of these China Eggs. You might drop it, and it is a valuable egg! But if you drop the China Egg and it breaks, the value is gone.

This is really stinking thinking.

Let me continue a crazy story from earlier to illustrate why.

In Chapter 3 (about matching products to markets), I began a story about a strange referral I once received. The referrer called me and gave me all the prospect's details, but told me that I could not use his name. And what good is a referred prospect if you cannot use the referrer's name?

But the prospect sounded so good that I had to call him anyway. On the call I had to fumble around: "You know, I cannot remember the guy's name that told me to give you a call. But I am going to be over in your town next week, late in the week. I wonder if I could just drop in to see you at your office, maybe Thursday around eleven o'clock?" He replied, "Sure. Come on by—I will be here all day."

And that is where I left off in chapter three. Kind of cruel, I know, but I will tell you the rest of the story now.

When I arrived, this prospect brought me into his office and we sat down. Looking straight at me, he said, "Roger, before we start talking, I need to tell you something."

"What is that?"

"I am totally uninsurable. I have a fatal disease."

At that moment, it was almost hard to keep from laughing. First off I could not use the referrer's name with the lead, and then upon meeting the guy I learn he is totally uninsurable. Well this is some life insurance lead, is not it? If you know anything about life insurance, you understand what a predicament this was.

He continued, "I do have a fair amount of insurance."

"Do you have the policies here, or are they in the bank's vault?"

"No, I have the policies in a safe right here."

"Well, since I am here and have the time, why not bring the policies to me? I will take a look."

He brought his policies out in a big box. Stunned, I saw that he had thirty-two life insurance policies that he had purchased before he found out about his disease.

The total face value of those policies was over nine million dollars!

As we talked, I discovered that he was personally worth about 50 million dollars. His wealth was all in rental properties, and he desired that his heirs not have to sell any properties in order to pay the estate taxes upon his death. That is why he owned so much life insurance. But he needed a total of 20 million dollars.

What would you do?

As an agent, what would you do in that situation?

Finishing up my notes on all the policies, I said to him, "Sir, you truly do need an audit. Many of these policies are very old. On some you are still paying premiums, though it is unnecessary that you keep paying. Others need the premium payments to continue. These thirty-two policies require a lot of work. You need a complete audit. That entails a lot of correspondence with the insurance companies to get it all straight.

"Here is what I will do for you. Normally I charge $100 per policy for an audit. You have 32 policies. I will charge you $3,000 and do the complete audit."

By the look on his face, I could tell that he was not interested. Frankly, he was not a money waster. He was what some people would call *cheap*.

I said, "I can tell by the look on your face you do not want to pay me that fee."

"You are right."

"So if I do not charge you the fee, what is in it for me?"

"Well, I am sure there will be some more insurance business here. I will make every effort to steer it your way."

(Pay close attention here—this is the most important thing I said to him during our entire conversation.)

"Sir, I will do the audit without the fee, on one condition. You will allow me to call all of these insurance companies on the telephone and identify myself as you. This is because in twenty minutes on the telephone, I can obtain more information than I would be able to in three months of letter writing."

"Okay. How are they going to know on the phone that you are me?"

"It is simple. They will ask me several questions: how to spell your name, which is right on the policy. The policy number, which is also on the policy. Your Social Security number, which is on the policy application. Your address and so forth. When I give them that information, they will let me ask them anything. If you allow me to do that, I can short-circuit this audit. The time investment will drop from months and months to a couple of weeks."

He agreed, and I performed the audit. Remember that he had nine million dollars' worth of life insurance. The cash value of these policies was near $4 million. And he was paying $200,000 in premiums to carry all these policies.

If you deal with estate taxes at all, there is a very simple fact that you had better know.

An individual can defer the estate taxes payable on his death until the death of his spouse. Now, this guy was supposedly totally uninsurable. He had a much, much shorter life expectancy than his wife. She had three things in her favor: (1) She was younger than him. (2) She was a female, and females on average live longer than males. (3) She was in perfect health.

I did something crazy. There is a rare insurance concept called a *viatical settlement*. Rarely do you hear ads for these on radio or TV, but they are still around. Basically, if you are an older person and no longer want to pay premiums on your life insurance policy, you can sell it to a company that offers viatical settlements. In exchange for paying you a lump sum now, the company receives the full policy value upon the death of the insured.

I found a company that would buy this man's policies. He owned $9 million of life insurance with near $4 million of cash value. The company paid him well over $6 million for the $9 million in policies, in advance of his death. At the time he was able to make that transaction tax free—so his assets went from $4 million of cash value to over $6 million of real cash, overnight. The $2 million gain was 100% tax free.

Then I took the $6 million of cash and bought a $20 million single-premium life insurance policy on his wife, so that the estate taxes could be paid at her death.

When all the transactions were finished, he went from $9 million of life insurance to $20 million, while reducing his $200,000 of premiums to $0. And his worth increased over $2 million.

Do you think he sent me a few referred leads? You bet he did!

In addition to the $20 million policy on his wife, I also wrote a total of $20 million on his kids. Four kids, $5 million each. So I wrote a total of $40 million in life insurance policies on this family. Pretty good result from an "uninsurable" referral!

In cases like these, keep plunging forward. You never know what you will discover. Consult your peers and managers. The most advantageous ideas often hide from view, and others can help you discover them.

This prospect was definitely a China Egg. In order to get his business, I had to actually pick up the phone and call him. Like I always say, "If you never call them you will never see them. If you never see them you will never sell them."

When the referrer hung up, I did not even set the phone down. I immediately dialed the prospect's number and started talking to him. I did not wait five seconds because I wanted to make or break this prospect immediately. Thinking about it might cause anxiety.

Making that call is one of the smartest things I did in my entire career.

Mental barriers block so many people from calling the prospect. They get a referral and start thinking about it. Unfortunately, they have stinking thinking–so the longer they wait the worse it becomes. They think, "He is the company president and drives a BMW. I drive a VW!"

Realize that these people have needs too. And they probably have a bunch of product pushers bugging them. You can be the solution provider they need.

You must conquer fear of making the initial call. I recommend that you dial the phone immediately. Make the call to that China Egg as soon as you can. Otherwise, you will talk yourself out of it. You will be so scared of the prospect disqualifying you that you disqualify yourself first, by not even making the call!

Moving on the prospect immediately is imperative. This is especially true with referral prospects—if you wait you may be a day short and a dollar late. All of a sudden the prospect will be meeting with someone else: "Look, I am already doing business with another agent. It is too late." As soon as you possibly can, make the call.

After you bite the bullet a few times and make the call, it will become second nature. Especially if you are blessed with a good sale, you will learn the lesson that sooner is always better. When you get a referral phone call, you will hardly be able to wait to hang up so you can dial the prospect. Your entire outlook will shift. That can change your career, because it will give you a confidence that you have never had before.

China Eggs have massive value—but also massive needs. The temptation is to think that the China Egg's insurance needs are all solved; thus, they must not need you. That is a lie. Until you get close to people and learn about them, you will never discover their true total need. Even if they themselves do not have a huge need, their parents or brother or uncle might. Maybe the family is wealthy, and you are talking to one brother, but the other brother has four times as much money and you sell a huge policy to him. Landing these huge prospects starts with simply trying.

But what if you try and fail?

"If at first you do not succeed, try, try again."

You may have an interview with a prospect that does not go anywhere. For some reason, it just does not work out.

The appointment was not as smooth as you had anticipated, and you do not sell them.

That does not mean the game is over. It does not mean that at all! Close the first interview by saying, "I am going to keep my eyes open for possible solutions to the issues we have been discussing. If something pops up, do you mind if I give you a call or send you an email?" The reply will always be, "Sure, that is fine." The prospect gets to easily end the interview, but you have left the door open for later on.

Do not be afraid to call a prospect again later on, especially if the prospect's circumstances have changed. For instance, you meet with Mr. Jones. Although you do not make the sale, you leave the door open for the future. Six months later you learn that Mr. Jones has merged his business with Mr. Smith's business, so now they are Smith and Jones. New opportunity! With two owners, a buy-and-sell arrangement should be insured. It is a brand new reason to return.

If you left the door ajar during the first meeting instead of slamming it shut, you can go to Mr. Jones and say: "Mr. Jones, you and I talked six months ago about such-and-such. Now that you and Mr. Smith have merged your business, there is another idea I would like to share with you two. It will only take a few minutes. Could we meet together, or maybe have lunch sometime?"

After Mr. Jones agrees, you have another opportunity to make a sale. So even if your China Egg falls off the shelf, all your horses and all your men may be able to put it together again.

NEVER BURN BRIDGES

If you cannot make a sale, make a friend.

Any good salesperson knows to leave the door open for a future presentation. Relationships have value, even if you do not make the sale.

I remember one fellow whom I visited several times, trying to sell him a policy. For whatever reason, it did not work out. But some time later, because of our friendly discussions, this fellow introduced me to a friend of his. Turns out his friend's needs were ten times larger! I sold him a policy that solved those needs and made a tidy commission. Though I was not able to sell the original fellow a policy, the relationship we established ended up being worth far more.

Record notes about your relationships in a special reference file. I always say that relationships are better than paychecks, because they keep on paying and paying.

Here is an example. Early in my career I called on an advertising agency. The agency was young, but very successful. The owner was a really tall chap, about 6 feet and 5 inches—a very impressive looking person. I stumbled into the agency and sold them group medical insurance. They took a liking to me, so I would go in occasionally and help them with any type of claim. I ended up writing all of the key man insurance, and all of the officers' personal life insurance. I think I insured everyone at the agency in one way or another.

One day the advertising agency's vice president called me into his office. He announced to me, "Roger, I need to tell you something."

"Sure, Jack. What is it?"

"Well, after all these years, I am leaving the agency. Our largest client has made me a job offer, and I am taking it."

I told him that I was surprised, but happy for him. Shortly thereafter he moved to Fort Lauderdale, Florida to take the job with the largest Oldsmobile dealer in the state.

Where do you suppose I went after Jack joined the Oldsmobile dealership? I went to see my buddy Jack, of course.

And who was my next big customer? Yes, it was the owner of the Oldsmobile dealership.

Do not burn bridges. Keep those doors open, because your contacts might bring you more prospects later on. In this case, an employee switched jobs and basically invited me in. You never know where a relationship might take you.

Lots of people find this difficult. When a customer moves away or switches jobs, they will virtually write that person off. Few things are worse than writing off an old customer. If they die with no living family, I give you permission to write them off. Other than that, do not forget them. You never know when they will bring you more value.

Establishing solid relationships is such a powerful concept. Do whatever you can to make and keep good fiends. If you can help someone outside of the insurance realm, by all means do it! If they invite you to volunteer for a cause they care about some Saturday morning, try to participate. If you help them out, they will never forget it. Their insurance guy cared enough to come and help!

One last time: Never burn bridges. Because if you burn a bridge, the people who get singed will not have something real nice to say about you.

SECTION IV.

PRINCIPLES OF SALES

CHAPTER 15.

DO UNTO OTHERS

"Do unto others as you would have them do unto you."
– Jesus

Put others first. Every agent I speak with, I advise them to do something significant to benefit others. If possible, help your prospect out. Not because it will bring you more business—because it is the right thing to do.

Of course, doing the right thing will often bring you more business than selfishly focusing on Number One. I discovered this as never before years ago when I lived in Florida.

The mayor of Fort Lauderdale at the time was a close personal friend and a client. He told me that the city's pension plan was completely in the clutches of a life insurance company. As a matter of fact, this life insurance company handled the pensions for virtually the entire east coast of Florida.

The mayor asked me, "Roger, will you do me a favor? I am going to form a pension committee for the city of Fort Lauderdale. Because I know you well and you are my insurance man, I want you to be the chairman. Other members of the committee will include the chief of police, the fire chief, some councilmen, and a two stock brokers."

It was a very impressive list of people, and I was the young kid. Fortunately, I knew the business very, very well.

Imagine yourself as an employee of the City of Fort Lauderdale. You are 30 years old. On your one-year work anniversary, the city buys a life insurance policy on your life. Every time you receive a salary increase, the city buys another life insurance policy to keep stacking the money up. Once you reach age 65, all the policies are cashed in. The cash is put into an annuity, and you then receive a check each month for the rest of your life. That is your pension.

I hate to say this, but a pension plan is absolutely no place for life insurance. If you want life insurance on employees, buy group life insurance—not expensive whole life insurance that will be intentionally lapsed before death.

Additionally, this whole life insurance only earned 2.5% interest. But because of the front-end sales charges, the policy did not realize any interest for nearly 10 years. So you might receive a policy at age 30, but you gain no interest until you turn 40. Then between age 40 and age 65 you accumulate money for retirement.

With my software, it was easy for me to run some calculations. We determined what would happen if the city restarted their pension plan: not buying more life insurance, but instead investing in Series E bonds.

Now that dates me. Series E bonds were the number-one-selling government bond type during World War II. Called "Victory Bonds," they were still available for purchase years after the war ended. The year I was on the committee, Series E bonds were paying 5% interest. Contrast that with this life insurance, where the average employee was lucky to get 2% interest.

The result? Two-and-a-half times as much money from the pension plan. What do you think that did for the city of Fort Lauderdale?

The time came for a huge meeting in front of the city commission. The meeting was public and it was televised, so you had all kinds of people attending. The insurance company's president and vice president were there, along with two senior actuaries.

I proved my calculations to them. If the city stopped dumping money into life insurance and invested in Series E bonds instead, it would save $25-30 million over the next 20 years.

After I concluded my presentation, the mayor stood up and opened the floor for questions. One nicely-dressed man walked up to the microphone and introduced himself. He said, "My name is Mr. C. I am a principal at the pension actuarial firm of A, B, and C. While I do not have a question for Mr. Gertz, I do have a comment about his presentation."

He continued very slowly. "Mr. Gertz's presentation was not correct."

Pause. "It was precisely correct!", he added.

"As he knows–and is probably chuckling under his breath–his presentation was actually very, very conservative. We calculate that by making his recommended change, the city could save not $25-30 million but $40-50 million."

After that commentary, the committee voted to change the pension plan according to my recommendation. The same pension actuary approached me afterward and said, "I am really kind of embarrassed. For over two years, we have been trying to make the city understand this waste. It took a young 30-year-old kid an hour to accomplish what we could not."

A humongous dinner was hosted, and I got to meet everyone involved in the decision. In the months following, the pension actuary and his firm sent me so much business I never had to look for a prospect the rest of my career in Fort Lauderdale.

Why did I benefit so much? Because I did unto others. I did not get paid a penny for the work I did for the city of Fort Lauderdale. Yet I was repaid in truckloads. That experience woke me up. It taught me a lesson: it revealed the importance of doing the right thing for people.

That was a big story. Let me end this chapter with a small one. This experience is even closer to my heart. When I first got in the business, I sold a fraternity brother of mine named Ed, a $25,000 policy. He got married a year or so later. Learning that they could not have children biologically, they adopted three kids. Obviously, as a married man, Ed needed more life insurance to protect his family. I called him and said, "Ed, you just do not have enough life insurance. With only $25,000 on you, you cannot afford to be dead very long. You need a bundle of life insurance."

"Yeah, I figured. What should I do?"

"You need $500,000 of real low-cost term insurance." I knew that would fit his budget, because he was doing very well.

He agreed and I got him the $500,000 policy. A year later, he was using his pickup truck to tow a sailboat with a tall metal mast. The mast hit an electric line, and Ed was instantly electrocuted. At the funeral, one of my friends remarked to me that I did not have anything to be embarrassed about. The policy I secured for Ed provided financial stability for his family during that difficult time. I will see Ed in heaven someday. He will probably say, "Whew. I am glad you got me that policy." I knew he needed more life insurance to protect his family, and I sold him what I would have purchased myself.

To wrap this up, remember: Do unto others what you would have them do unto you. That is the biblical saying, and it is a good one to follow.

CHAPTER 16

LOOK FOR NEEDS

A number of years ago, the brother of one of my agents co-owned a very successful business in a nearby town. One day the agent and I were in this town, so we had lunch with the brother and his partner. Both these men were fairly young and appeared to be in perfect health.

During casual conversation, these two partners mentioned that they kept a rather large—I would say enormous—amount of money at a local bank. I curiously inquired, "Why do you keep such a large amount of money at the bank?"

One of the partners replied, "I do not know. We have been successful, and the money has piled up there. It works out because the banker knows we are doing well. If we need a short-term loan, we can get it in a matter of minutes. So it helps our relationship with the bank."

I then asked a question that changed everything.

"Did the bank ever share with you how to significantly increase the return on your deposits, and at the same time enjoy a huge amount of life insurance without additional expense? And how the life insurance could be used to fund a buy-and-sell agreement between you two, all with the same dollars?"

They had me repeat the statement three times. Puzzlement was apparent on their faces. They said, "Let us get this straight. You are asking me if the bank ever shared with us an idea of how to increase our returns?"

"Yes—and at the same time enjoy a huge amount of life insurance."

"Well, they are not in the life insurance business."

"True. But I want you to know something. If you ever saw the financial statements of Bank of America and Wells Fargo, you would be rather started to discover that both those banks possess multi-billions (not millions, *billions*) of dollars of assets in life insurance policies.

"The banker never told you this because the banker pays you a low rate of interest. Then they turn around and invest your money at a higher rate of interest in bank loans, bonds, or with a life insurance company—at virtually no risk. They also use the policies' excess benefits to insure their key employees.

"Once I get back to the office today, I will take a few minutes and put something together. Then we can meet for coffee sometime soon. The proposal will show you how you can move some money sideways from the bank to a life insurance company—and double or triple your return. Two other benefits are that you pay no taxes on the money as it grows and that this provides you with a big pile of extra life insurance to fund a buy-and-sell agreement.

"Now, I want to take just a minute to explain buy-and-sell agreements. Nothing could be more important between two partners, even if they are blood brothers. In that situation, it might be even more important. Two partners need to have an agreement in writing: should one of them die prematurely, the surviving partner will buy the deceased partner's share of the business. So the widow would receive money to live off of, and the surviving partner can continue to operate the business. This agreement is critical.

"What if I could show you a way to fund a buy-and-sell agreement without cost you any money out-of-pocket? Would that interest you?

Sometimes we do not realize power of the financial products available to us. I will put it on paper to explain it further, and you are going to like what you see."

A few days later we met again and I answered their questions. We ended with a very substantial sale, a $100,000 single-premium policy on each partner. They were young enough that the single-premium included a $400,000 policy on each of them to fund the Buy-and-Sell Agreement.

The sale began when I asked a few subtle questions during lunch. Those key questions exposed a huge need.

With two partners, a buy-and-sell agreement is always on my mind. Years ago, I helped two business partners fund such an agreement using life insurance. Shortly afterward one partner was killed. The life insurance absolutely saved the business, and the jobs of the dozen employees. The surviving partner said to me, "Roger, that life insurance saved the business. These employees do not totally understand it, but that is truly what happened. I cannot thank you enough for bring this need to our attention." I replied, "You are welcome. A buy-and-sell agreement is one of the basics of business, and it is my job to think about such things. Because sometimes the worst happens."

When you are out to lunch with a potential prospect, you must listen. Let ideas flow though your mind. Might there be a need? If there is a genuine need, cost will rarely be a barrier. Life insurance for healthy people is extremely inexpensive.

Notice that I hardly mentioned the life insurance product during lunch. The entire discussion focused around transferring dollars from a low-return investment to a high-return investment. In a way, the transition was from one bank to another. But at the Bank of Life Insurance, we gained the advantage of a life insurance policy to go along with the larger return.

When I tell this story, people often ask me to explain a buy-and-sell agreement further. It can be likened to a will, which is another type of agreement. A will is your agreement with your heirs to give them your money and possessions. If I am a widower with one son, and I will everything to him, at my death the will is probated and my son receives title to all my assets. It is as simple as that.

A buy-and-sell agreement is an agreement between two business partners. Upon the death of one partner, the agreement stipulates that the surviving partner will buy out the deceased partner's interest.

Over the years I have been in several partnerships: the last thing I want is to end up in business with my deceased partner's widow. It is nothing against her personally. She might be a great friend of the family, but virtually never is she equipped to run the business. She lacks the background, experience, and knowledge that her husband possessed. Plus, she probably does not want to take on the responsibility of co-owning a business. The best solution for me—and for her—is that I buy my partner out, ensuring a clean break.

If you are in business with a partner, you need a buy-and-sell agreement. In particular, I recommend you look at a Specimen Buy-and-Sell agreement. Most insurance agents will have one. You can probably also find one online for free by searching Google for "specimen buy-and-sell agreement." Print it out, make some notes, and take it to your attorney. Ask him to clean it up and execute it. That will save his time, and thus your money.

If you understand the different needs people have, and know how to offer solutions winningly, you will find it easier than ever to make simple business sales.

CHAPTER 17

BE A BANK ROBBER

Do you want to be a bank robber?

I know, that is a funny way to title a chapter. But recall the quote I used to open this book.

Sheriff: "Why do you rob banks?"

Jesse James: "Because that is where the money is."

Like Jesse, I am going to teach you how to rob banks. Unlike Jesse, I will show you how to do it legally.

As you read the story, keep yourself from becoming too enmeshed in the details. I share this story not so you will copy my strategy exactly. In fact, you may not ever face a situation exactly like this during your career.

Rather, I aim to inspire you to find your own innovative solutions. Use your industry knowledge to help people–or even to solve needs they never knew they had.

One day I was meeting with a good friend over lunch. This friend was the president of a small local bank, and in the course of our conversation we got into a discussion of his benefit package. He told me that his fringe benefit package was excellent; however, the one weak aspect was his pension plan. I told my friend, "I have an idea. Based on what you have told me, I believe Uncle Sam can add a million dollars to your retirement account, at no cost to your bank. Would you be interested in looking at that?" He responded, "Yes! I would be very interested."

The precise funding details are a bit complicated. If you want the full rundown, give me a call or shoot me an email. My contact information is at the end of this book.

Here is the short version. Banks can borrow money from the federal government–called "Fed Funds." If the bank needs a pile of money in order to make a huge loan, they can borrow from the government at a very low interest rate.

Back when I was meeting with this friend, life insurance companies were paying about 6% interest. Moreover, the life insurance grows tax free: when the insured dies, all taxes are forgiven.

So the bank could simply borrow from the government and pay only 1% interest, then turn around and invest that money in life insurance with a 6% return. The bank's return on investment would enable them to give my friend an extra million dollars over the course of his retirement. And then the bank would recoup every penny when he passed away, because of the tax-free death benefit.

When I finished explaining this to my friend, he said to me, "Roger, I want you to come and present this to my Board of Directors. And I do not let people speak to them often: you will be only the second to ever do so."

The next week I delivered the presentation. At the end, one of the members of the board stood up to comment. He said, "I have been on this board for 20 years. If we fail to do this for our bank president–who has been with the bank since high school and served us for many years–I will resign from the board, because we are a bunch of idiots."

Sure enough, the board overwhelmingly chose to follow my recommendation. They loved having this guy as the bank president, because he was a local guy. Actually, he started working at the bank during high school. He went to college, kept working at the bank, and eventually became the bank president. He was a local hero, a great guy, with a family everyone loved. When I provided them with a way to repay the bank president for all the good work he had done, they jumped at it.

As a bonus for me, it ended up being a huge sale. So huge that I negotiated a special commission from the insurance company. Normally most all of the commission is paid out on the front end, but I did not want it all at the beginning. I said to the insurance company president, "I want to spread this large commission out."

"Roger, I do not exactly know how to do that. I understand what you mean, but I do not understand how to make that happen."

"Okay. Get the actuary on the phone. You have his number there, and he will probably figure it out while we are on the phone with him."

We called the actuary and explained the situation. He told us, "Give me a day or so. What Roger wants to do can be done, but I want to have some people check it out and make sure we get the numbers right."

Every year, I am paid a renewal commission on that huge chunk of money. In fact, it is large enough that I have the company pay it out quarterly. I enjoy getting the check every three months rather than waiting until year-end. I will keep on receiving checks until the bank president dies. It is a pretty nice renewal commission. I mean, it took me an hour to make the sale. Over the years, my commissions on that one sale have now totaled over $150,000.

Again, I simply offered a solution. Do the same with your clients. Look out for others and see what happens.

CHAPTER 18.

LITTLE THINGS COUNT

You probably know the phrase, "It is the little things that count." And it is true. If you want more referrals, know that your clients will refer prospects to you more frequently if you do the little things.

Stories of little things that count are endless. When you see someone in need, stop and help them. Recently I heard a story on TV about a man who stopped to help change a flat tire on a limousine. The rich couple inside asked what they could do for him, and he just asked them to send flowers to his wife. Sure enough, the rich couple sent flowers–with a note saying, "We paid off your mortgage too." That is a huge thing that came from a very small thing. What a story.

#1. Send a Gift

Consider sending a gift to anyone who gives you a referral. This is an encouragement for them to send more!

Remember I told you that I am a Starbucks junkie. On my last birthday, I actually received two surprise birthday parties. One was on my actual birthday, and the other was a few days beforehand at Starbucks, held after church on Sunday.

The attendees gave me little cards and presents, but guess what I got the most of? Starbucks cards. At least half a dozen of them! Why? Because people know I like Starbucks. If they give me a Starbucks card I can buy coffee, or a sandwich, or whatever I want. Boy did I appreciate those cards!

The Starbucks card is a great choice for coffee addicts. If you want to gift the non-coffee-drinkers in your life too, check out the gift cards that are good for dinner at several different restaurants. The referrer will enjoy an evening out, and be thinking about you all the while.

If you place your gift inside a card, do not forget to write a note. A handwritten note means so much. Even if it is just, "Hey Roger, enjoy a cup of coffee! – Charlie." That is all it has to be. You do not need to write an epistle. A simple note tells the other person you are thinking about them, and that is what we crave. Knowing that others are thinking about us warms us up inside.

Email can do the job of a note, but it is not as warm. The other day I read an article about how many emails the average person sends and receives each day: 121. I would hate to look at my personal average. If I recorded all the emails I receive, plus all the emails that automatically go in my junk folder, I know it would be well over that. And about 95% of those emails belong in the junk pile, because they are cold emails. So you can send a thank-you note via email, but the recipient may view it as just another email to process.

Sending handwritten thank-you cards with a Starbucks gift card inside can change your life. Clients will refer you again, and again, and again. People call me and say, "I got your nice thank-you with the Starbucks card inside, and I really appreciate it." I reply, "You have been kind enough to send me referrals. It is the least I could do." Once a guy said back to me, "While we are on the topic, do you have a pen handy? Let me give you this guy's name. His name is Joe Smith, and he lives in such-and-such a neighborhood, and here is his phone number. I think he could use your help." Bingo, another referral.

#2. The More the Merrier

Another little thing is taking the few seconds to introduce people to one another. When you encounter a friend or prospect or client, if you have your spouses with you, be sure to make introductions. The more the merrier!

Forgive me for mentioning Starbucks again. But I have Starbucks friends whose wives are friends with my wife. While we guys are talking, the wives will meet and talk too. It deepens relationships all around.

Introduce people to others who might benefit them. That can be huge. Upon occasion I have made an introduction and heard about it later on: "Am I glad you introduced me to so-and-so! We ended up doing a bunch of business together." My youngest son is absolutely an expert in business development, and he uses this technique every day.

#3. Volunteer

Volunteering tells people that you really care. You did not have to help, but you chose to do it anyway. I cannot emphasize this too strongly. As a life insurance agent, over the years I have earned the trust of many prospects and client by volunteering and serving alongside them.

#4. Be Fast

Do not hesitate to do little things. Be fast. When you meet someone, shoot them a quick email a couple hours later. Say, "Hey Joe, it was great to meet you earlier today. I look forward to keeping in touch." Few people take the time to do that. You will set yourself apart.

If the person you met did you a favor, follow up a few days later with the thank-you-and-Starbucks-card routine. You will get a double-header from that! Out of all the people I have dealt with in my career–literally thousands of people at this point–I will never forget those who really went the extra mile and helped me. I will never forget them for that.

#5. Learn the Lingo

Early in my career, I was sending a lot of direct mail to doctors. Pretty soon I knew the lingo and could speak "doctor language." When you are around a group of people regularly, try to pick up on their industry jargon. You might even speak it a bit. Employ their lingo sparingly, but use it when it counts.

When you say something using their business language, they know you have been listening to them.

My son is such an expert at this. He can talk to someone about their business for 15 minutes, then speak the lingo as though he had been in the industry for 20 years. For him, it is a gift. For the rest of us, it is a learned skill.

Your Turn

Now it is your turn. Time to use your imagination. Grab a piece of paper and take a break from reading this book. Resolve to sit and think for 15 minutes about little things you could do to make others' lives brighter. Remember opportunities you have missed and then regretted. Now it is too late to fix them, but you can still contemplate them and not make the same mistake again. Add joy to others' lives, starting today.

SECTION V.

POSITIONING YOURSELF TO SUCCEED

BUILD RELATIONSHIPS (AT STARBUCKS)

Technology has revolutionized the life insurance industry. And I am not just talking about big corporations. I am talking about you. The power of technology enables you to sell more effectively no matter where you are. Including Starbucks!

Let me tell you a story. I am a Starbucks junkie—I love their coffee and go there virtually every day. I sit with friends, and we have fun and a light time. The scene is always just perfect.

This morning, a gentleman I know at Starbucks asked me about life insurance. We got on the topic because of crossword puzzles. Solving crossword puzzles is a shared hobby of ours, and I was stuck on my puzzle. He figured out a couple words for me, then I solved the last word. We kept talking, and I told him a short story from my career—which of course involved life insurance. That triggered him to ask me his life insurance question:

"I am a little confused about my life insurance policy. I know you are in that business."

"What are you confused about?"

He made a couple statements about his policy that seemed strange to me. We had talked many times in the past, so he was not a cold call at all. He was warm and happy to chat. So I said to him, "Do you have a copier at home?"

"Oh, sure."

"Great. When you go home this evening, grab your policy and make a copy of the front page. Normally that contains your name, your age, the amount of insurance, the company name, and a description of the policy. Bring the copy in to me tomorrow, and I will see if I can answer your questions."

"I will be happy to do that."

That turned into a nice sale.

Our entire encounter was devoid of pressure. He was uncomfortable about his policy statement, concerned that it would lapse or run out. But I did not say anything uncomfortable to him. I kept it casual. What is uncomfortable about making a copy of your policy and giving it to someone you trust?

Noticing his age, one of my other questions was, "Now that you are a senior and your kids are grown, do you really need any life insurance?" He responded, "Yes, I probably do. My wife and I are raising one of our grandchildren." Interesting situation. It is becoming more frequent these days: retired seniors raising a six-year-old child. This man has a definite need for life insurance, and he became a prospect out of the people I see frequently at Starbucks.

This sort of thing happens to me frequently. Several months ago, I was sitting at Starbucks gazing out the front windows. The view includes four banks: one to the left, two across the street, and one to the right. I visit those banks all the time, so I mentioned something to my friend sitting next to me. I told him that after coffee, I needed to go across to the bank and make a deposit on my way home. He commented, "Banks these days sure do not offer much to the depositor, besides a checking account."

"Yeah, I agree. They are paying almost nothing in interest nowadays. In the old days, we used to shoot for accumulating a million dollars and putting it in the bank. If the banks were paying 6% interest annually, we would get $60,000 each year. Along with Social Security, that money would allow us to live comfortably. Remember those days?"

"Yeah, they sure are not around anymore."

"You got a minute? Let me show you something." Taking out my smartphone, I selected a software app that my programmer created for me. The app illustrates how a single premium life insurance policy works. Issued by a good-sized fraternal life insurance company, this policy is a very fine product.

The policy illustration is beautiful. The key: it is not a bunch of numbers in columns. That is boring, ugly, and quite hard to understand. Instead, the illustration is different-colored bar charts. A red bar shows the growth of the bank deposit. A blue bar shows the growth of the life insurance's cash value. A green bar shows the total amount of life insurance. All this in one neat graphic! It all appears on my iPhone screen, no scrolling necessary. Plus, I can change any data input with the push of a button. (You can see this graphic on the next page.)

So I took out my iPhone and said, "Let me ask you a question. I hate to be nosy, but do you have quite a bit of money in the bank over there?"

"Yes, several hundred thousand dollars, he answered."

"Great. To make this illustration really simple, let me show you the growth of a $100,000 life insurance policy compared with $100,000 in the bank. First, I have to ask you a really personal question. How old are you?"

After getting his age, I moved on. Now we can run the numbers. So we put $100,000 in the bank for you, and assume the bank is paying out 0.5% interest each year. I press the button and look–the red bar goes up. Twenty years down the road, your $100,000 in the bank has grown to $108,311.

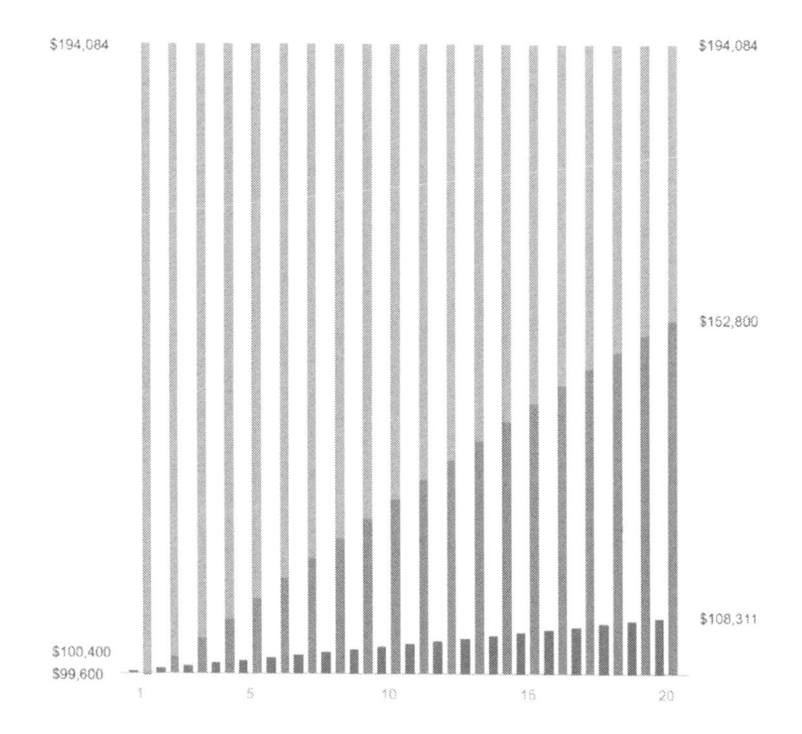

"Now check out the blue bars. If you put $100,000 in this life insurance policy, the cash value grows in twenty years to $152,800. Guaranteed. And then the death benefit–shown as green bars–will be worth $194,084 to your family. Whereas the money in the bank would be worth only $108,000.

"Do you want to be Mr. Red Bar, or Mr. Blue and Green Bar?"

He said, "Oh my goodness. What do I have to do to get this policy?"

"You have to answer a few medical questions. That is about it. And assuming you pass the medical exam and they issue the policy, we have to go across the street to the bank and get $100,000."

"Bring the paperwork in tomorrow. We will get started."

Remember what I said in chapter 11 about not looking like a salesperson? Prospects are everywhere. You just have to strike up a conversation. Have coffee and build relationships.

This also ties into the social tips in chapter 9. Genuinely care about other people. Make a friend. Too many salespeople are stressed out because they feel they have to do a formal sales presentation. Relax. Be real and be interested. Encountering the opportunity to make a sale, pull out your iPhone and use the visual policy app.

Selling at Starbucks is simple when you have the right tools. The graphic illustration communicated more clearly than ice-cold columns of numbers ever could.

You can get this software app for yourself, if you want. The app is part of my main business: providing software to insurance companies to help them sell their products more quickly and more easily. That app illustration compared to what you would normally see–it is 10 times as powerful. To learn more, visit www.VisCalc.com and select the "Illustration Software" tab in the top navigational bar. You can sell anywhere, if you have the tools and techniques.

Build relationships and you will see your business increase. My daily visits to Starbucks over the years have created many relationships, and sooner or later those people need life insurance help. When they have a need, I am there to help.

You can do the same. Starbucks does not have to be your location of choice. Spend time at a restaurant, a gym, a club, or any other public place. Build relationships and be ready to serve.

CHAPTER 20

THE SOFTWARE ADVANTAGE

Have you ever been tax audited?

It is not a fun experience. I will never forget the first time I was audited. I kept records well, but oh my goodness—by the time I went to the audit I had a gym bag full of receipts.

The auditor told me, "I do not audit gym bags full of receipts. You have to put all that data in some kind of report, like a spreadsheet."

I had to go back to my office and spend three ugly days with my secretary—practically the entire eight hours each day—reading off receipts while she typed them into a spreadsheet. After we finished I took the spreadsheet to the audit, and I was out in 30 minutes. The auditor told me, "You did a very good job. You are going to get a letter from the IRS accepting your tax return as you filed it."

On my way back I said to myself, "That is never going to happen to me again." Arriving at the office, I went to my programmer: "Doug, grab your legal pad. I have just thought of an idea for a new program."

"Is this some kind of insurance or annuity program or something?"

"Nope. And I have already named it."

"What is the name?"

"April 15th."

He started to laugh. "You just came from that tax audit, right?"

"Yep. I am never going to let that happen to me again."

So we wrote the software program titled "April 15th."

Here is how it works. I open the program and enter my mileage for the day. I enter my expense receipts. And that is it for the day. Then every month I grab my bank statement and mark all the items I do not have receipts for. I enter all of those items into the program, and bingo. Done for the month.

At the end of the year I press the button and everything is in order. Filing my tax return takes me 20 minutes.

The next time I got audited, I was prepared. The IRS auditor asked me, "How did you get this information organized so well?"

"I track everything in a software program called April 15th."

"April 15th...I have never heard of that."

"Well, you are talking to the program's author."

"I have never seen records so crisp and clean and clear. What is your intention with this program? What are you going to do with it?"

"My intention is to put the IRS out of business."

He looked at me kind of funny. I said, "Can I get a little laugh out of you?" He started to chuckle, and I explained how my first audit was so horrible it inspired me to create this program.

I have thousands of users for April 15th. People have used it for years and years, because it is such a simple program. Recently I was talking with a friend of mine, the business manager for one of the fraternal insurance agencies I work closely with. He is aware of my software programs, and he uses a bunch of them. I said to him, "John, are you using April 15th to track all of your business expenses?"

"No, Roger, I have not started using that."

"John, you have given me that reply for the last two years. I really feel bad for you with tax day coming up. You have all your work ahead of you, while I file my taxes every day. Entering my expenses into this simple program takes me seconds. If you do not start using this program, when tax time comes around you are going to miss 40% of the deductions you should have taken. I am mailing you a website link right now. Do you see it in your email?"

"Yes, I see it."

"Click on it. Now go to www.Join.me. Start a meeting, give me the code, and I will be able to view your screen. I will walk you through the program. You are going to hear how to operate the software from the author."

The walkthrough took a mere five minutes. He said, "Oh my goodness. I never realized it was so easy."

I replied, "John, I could not live without this."

And I was not exaggerating. I really could not live and operate my business without this software. Life insurance agents are independent businessmen, 1099 salesmen. At the end of the year you do not get a W-2 but a 1099. You are on your own. And if you are on your own as a businessperson, operating out of your home, so many things are deductible. I deduct repairs, furnishings, home maintenance, mortgage interest and more. Deduct, deduct, deduct.

Everything gets entered into April 15th. I carry a money clip around and put my receipts in it. Earlier today I had to empty it out, because I had missed entering my expenses into April 15th for a few days. The clip was bulging with receipts. There were at least six Starbucks receipts, two restaurant receipts, a Home Depot receipt, and a Staples receipt. I opened up April 15th and entered them all in a matter of seconds. I also entered the mileage and my destination. For instance, yesterday I went to the doctor, and that whole trip is deductible. The doctor's parking lot charged me $5, and that is deductible too. I am trying to deduct air, but I just have not figured out how yet.

This morning, another Starbucks friend thanked me for April 15th. She had been to her CPA yesterday, and she could not believe the amazing orderly reports April 15th created for her.

Having the right software gives you a humongous advantage.

CHAPTER 21

A SOFTWARE SELLING SOLUTION

The Family Needs Analysis is probably the most common basis for asking a prospect for an appointment to discuss life insurance. When I started in business many years ago with the Aetna Life Insurance Company, the other new salespeople and I were all sent up to Hartford, Connecticut to learn this type of presentation.

This analysis is so powerful that everyone should know how to use it, and so basic that anyone can learn to use it–but also so ignored that few people do use it.

To get this software selling solution for yourself, go to www.VisCalc.com and click the "Free Apps" tab. Then scroll to the Family Needs Analysis selection. Download the app, then view the user video. In minutes, you can become an expert in this powerful–yet superbly simple–application.

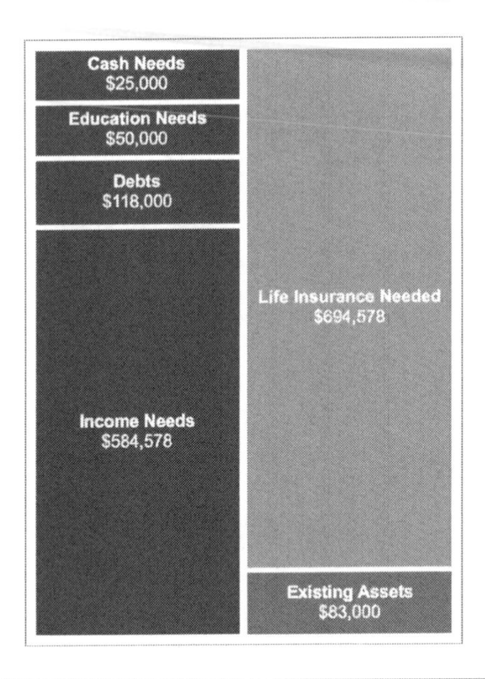
Cash Needs
$25,000
Education Needs
$50,000
Debts
$118,000
Income Needs
$584,578
Life Insurance Needed
$694,578
Existing Assets
$83,000

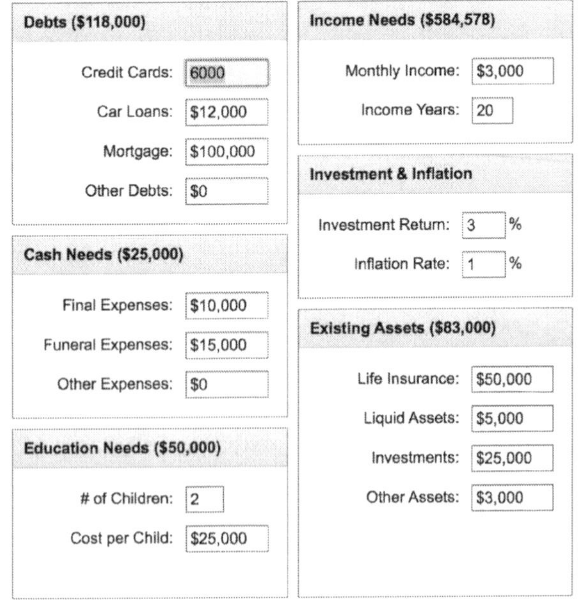
Debts ($118,000)
Credit Cards: 6000
Car Loans: $12,000
Mortgage: $100,000
Other Debts: $0
Cash Needs ($25,000)
Final Expenses: $10,000
Funeral Expenses: $15,000
Other Expenses: $0
Education Needs ($50,000)
# of Children: 2
Cost per Child: $25,000
Income Needs ($584,578)
Monthly Income: $3,000
Income Years: 20
Investment & Inflation
Investment Return: 3 %
Inflation Rate: 1 %
Existing Assets ($83,000)
Life Insurance: $50,000
Liquid Assets: $5,000
Investments: $25,000
Other Assets: $3,000

CONCLUSION

Thank you for taking time to read this book. I pray that it will help you in your career. These concepts have benefited many agents through my experience in presentations and personal conversations, so I am confident that they will benefit you too.

Identifying the right market will open up the bank vault for you. That is what I did when I started out in business. I identified my right market: professionals and business owners. Then I was able to withdraw as much money as I wanted from the bank vault, just by writing policies that served the needs of my clients. Because I was selling solutions, not products.

You can do the same thing. I hope that you use this book as a workbook and as a tool. Do not put this book on your bookshelf and let it collect dust. Go back and reread some chapters. Apply what you have learned.

Attempting to change everything at once may be overwhelming. So do one thing at a time. Do not let your mind stop you from taking a small step forward this very day.

I was not born a multimillion-dollar producer. I worked and achieved that status—you can too. In your hands you hold the blueprint to your dream career. Yes, it will take work. *But you can do it.* I believe you can do it.

Let me tell one last story. I vividly remember the first time I played baseball as an eight-year-old. A group of kids my age all went out to the playground, and I got up to bat. The pitcher lobbed the ball to me underhanded: Strike one! I missed by a mile. That is when I realized I had to really focus.

After a couple of swings, I hit the ball and ran to first base. Playing baseball for the first time ever, I got a hit! That is big.

One of my close friends was not nearly as impressed with me as I was. He said, "Roger, I need to tell you something. You are not batting properly."

"What do you mean?"

"Let me show you." He took the bat and walked into the batter's box. He showed me proper swinging technique. "Now you try it."

I stepped into the batter's box and took a swing. My friend said, "Roger, you are holding the bat cross-handed. Your left hand is on top of your right hand, and it should be the other way around."

Switching my hands around, I replied, "This feels weird. I am not comfortable batting with my right hand on top."

My friend was wiser than me. He said, "Okay. Stand on the other side of home plate, and try batting left-handed." Standing on the left-handers' side of the plate, I could have my left hand on top and still be in proper form. The pitcher lobbed the ball in again. I hit the first pitch!

Unbeknownst to me, I was a left-handed batter. But I had been batting right-handed and cross-handed (with the wrong hand on top). As soon as I was taught to bat left-handed, my baseball hitting ability skyrocketed.

Might you be batting right-handed and cross-handed?

I bet you have gotten some hits during your career. Maybe even some big ones. But batting incorrectly hampers your growth. You will never reach the major leagues with improper form.

This book is your insurance industry Batter's Handbook. I have explained proper form throughout these chapters. Now is the time for you to apply what you have learned.

Feel free to contact me with questions or comments. My name, email address, and website are below. I would love to hear how this book helped you succeed.

So be bold and bat left-handed. You will never become an All-Star by staying in the wrong side of the batter's box. But when you are positioned correctly, the sky is the limit.

One last thing. My website is www.VisCalc.com. Visit the site and click on the "Blog" tab—it contains many very helpful sales ideas. Each blog is archived, so you can go back through the previous blogs and pick my brain.

The old saying was, "It is yours for the picking." In today's tech world: "It is yours for the clicking."

Roger A. Gertz, CLU
rogergertz@gmail.com

ABOUT THE AUTHOR

Roger Gertz, CLU has been a successful life insurance agent, sales manager, and software developer for over fifty years. During those years he has been a multimillion-dollar producer, a developer of large sales teams, and a pioneer in the use of computer-generated sales illustrations and techniques.

In the sunset of his career, Roger and a young programming expert have developed a unique sales illustration format. His company name–VisCalc–tips you off to his specialty: visual life insurance illustrations. It has been proven by experts that a visual sales illustration is ten times as powerful as the ledger format agents commonly use.

While developing sales organizations, Roger learned that most agents receive little or no instruction in discovering and building market strategies. He was blessed to work with several huge personal producers and learn their techniques for growing successful careers. When Roger decided to spend the majority of his time creating computerized sales documents–primarily among fraternal life companies–he realized that this segment of the market was in need of assistance.

Roger's first fraternal venture was with a small company based in the northern United States that was considering a Universal Life plan. Interest rates were high and the product was sweeping the nation. Roger created the company's first software system, and also grew the company's leading agency in his first year with the company.

Fraternal agents generally spend a lot of time and effort selling small policies and tiny juvenile contracts, just to grow the membership. Roger found that fraternal companies were unique in several areas. They are generally religious, ethnic, or occupationally-based organizations that were formed many years ago. For decades they have enjoyed tax-exempt status. But they also have a unique asset: fellowship. The members of a fraternal company enjoy getting together like a family. They share a lot together: meetings, projects, dinners (and delicious recipes), sporting events (like bowling, golf and softball), and much more.

Many companies offer scholarships to members and their children. All this activity builds relationships for a lifetime, and Roger counts it a privilege to be a part.

Made in the USA
San Bernardino, CA
14 May 2016